Advances in Psychology Series

2

EARLY LEARNING IN MAN AND ANIMAL

IN THE SAME SERIES

Models of Thinking
F. H. GEORGE
Psychological Probability
JOHN COHEN

WITHDRAWN

W. SLUCKIN
Professor of Psychology, University of Leicester

Early Learning
in Man and Animal

London
GEORGE ALLEN AND UNWIN LTD
RUSKIN HOUSE · MUSEUM STREET

FIRST PUBLISHED IN 1970
SECOND IMPRESSION 1972

© *George Allen & Unwin Ltd., 1970*

ISBN 0 04 156001 9 cased
ISBN 0 04 156002 7 paper

PRINTED IN THE U.S.A.
in 10 on 12 pt. Times type

To Alice

PREFACE

I have set out in this slim volume to treat in a selective manner a number of topics in a field rather imprecisely described as early learning. The coverage is of uneven depth, reflecting both my special interests and patchy knowledge. However, readers interested in the developments concerning developmental psychology and allied disciplines may find of some value the research reviews and discussions presented in the ten chapters which follow.

An attempt to specify the first two words of the title should help in indicating the intended scope of the book. 'Early' refers to the first days or weeks after birth in fast-maturing species; but occasionally the first few months or years will be considered, especially in the slowly maturing species such as our own. 'Learning' is notoriously hard to define: it is difficult to separate it from the process of maturation, and it is somewhat uncertain when learning shades off into something loosely called experience. It will be seen that the conception of learning adopted in this book, while not the widest possible, is not so narrow as to be confined to what is traditionally described as conditioning. Perhaps it should be added that the word 'animals' will be used as an abbreviation for animals comprising only birds and mammals.

I am very grateful indeed for the help I have had from Derek Wright. He has read an earlier version of the entire MS and has made many pointed and constructive criticisms. Without these the book would have had many more weaknesses than it has now.

WLADYSLAW SLUCKIN
September 1969

CONTENTS

CHAPTER 1

Early and Later Learning

One of the centres of interest in modern psychology is the problem of the significance of early learning. Learning, in a broad sense, is regarded by many as peculiarly important in infancy. Learning at that stage of development is thought to be laying the foundations for the individual's characteristic behaviour later in life. Yet it is by no means self-evident that learning in infancy must be exceptionally influential. It may, in fact, be thought that infants, human and animal, learn but little, learn inefficiently, and forget quickly. However, debate at this level of generality is sterile: research findings can tell us little about the *general* importance of early learning; but they do tell us a great deal about the developmental significance of *particular* learning processes early in life. Even so, in the light of recent extensive animal and human studies, certain broad conclusions about the character of *behavioural development* may be reached. It is our aim to survey the salient research findings in this wide field, and to consider the extent of present-day understanding of early learning and its effects in both animals and man.

I. *Early learning and early experience*

Some types of research come under the heading of early learning while others are said to be concerned with early experience. Can a valid distinction be drawn between the two? When in everyday language we refer to early experiences, we are talking about the memory which we have of past events. If experiences are to be studied, they must be regarded as observable events, namely the effects of stimulation on the organism. (1) Early experience refers, then, to all effects of stimulation in infancy, both immediate and long-lasting. By contrast, the connotation of early learning is rather narrower; thus certain kinds of early experience involve no learning, although all early learning constitutes early experience.

Consider such environmental conditions as high or low temperatures. When continuously experienced early in life, these conditions may markedly influence the organism's physical development and consequently its later behaviour. However, such effects have little or nothing to do with early learning (and yet *changes* of temperature can act as rewards and punishments, and be instrumental in bringing about learning to approach and avoid certain features of the environment). Other experiences early in life, although they would not normally be described as learning, may well lie behind the acquisition of a variety of modes of behaviour. The experience of insufficiency of food, for instance, may be at the back of habitual persistent calling or searching for food later in life, and of other types of activity which would be atypical of individuals without some early experience of food deprivation. And then there are those early experiences that are quite manifestly conditioning or learning. Whenever, for example, a human or animal infant acquires a preference for some type of food as a result of pertinent experience, learning has occurred. Likewise, learning takes place when the young individual acquires ways of escaping from, or avoiding, painful situations.

The survival of the individual and species would be imperilled unless some learning took place early in life. However the young of altricial species, being initially immobile and helpless, and normally getting all the essential parental care in early infancy, may be expected to learn very little during the first stages of development. It is only somewhat later that failure to learn begins to carry a heavy penalty. The position is different in precocial species, that is, in those whose young have well-developed sense organs and are capable of locomotion soon after birth. If such young are to survive they must learn fairly quickly; at least, there are certain things which they are capable of learning and there is some urgency that they be learned. Passerine birds, rats, cats and dogs are examples of altricial animals; ground-nesting birds, sheep, cattle and horses are typical of precocial animals. Pigs and primates, including the human species, are altricial rather than precocial, but are physically sufficiently well developed at birth to be capable of some very early learning.

We shall not be concerned here with all early environmental influences, but only with those which, for one reason or another, may be said to produce early learning. And so certain experimental studies of later effects of early experience are outside the scope of this book, while others are of border-line interest or perhaps only just within our purview. To the latter categories belong investigations involving the handling or shocking of infant animals, such as mice and rats. In fact young animals so stimulated have been found to be less reactive later in life (it used to be said, less emotional) than control subjects. Does such stimulation entail early learning? The right answer may be semantic rather than substantive in character. Broadly conceived, learning would include effects of this kind; but whether it would be advisable to think of learning in such broad terms is a somewhat controversial matter. At any rate, we shall consider early experiences that are marginally learning much more briefly than early learning in the narrow sense. The reader will notice that we are not tackling the thorny problem of the definition of learning. The term 'learning' appears often to be used inconsistently even by learning theorists. It will be seen that, along with others who study aspects of learning empirically, we shall use the term in a descriptive way to refer to certain, but not all, changes of behavioural potentiality.

II. *Learning early and later in life*

As said earlier, the question as to whether early learning differs substantially from later learning may be too broad and too vague to be capable of eliciting a simple answer. In the first place it is uncertain what the criteria for assessing the differences between early and later learning should be. Secondly, any discernible differences may, of course, be characteristic of some species but not of others. Yet, the view that developmental changes in the character of learning are profound and that first learning differs sharply from later learning has been widely accepted.

The age factor had certainly been considered by early students of animal and human learning. The very early view was that young animals, though not those in their infancy, learn faster than older ones. Then in the late 1920s it was reported that such differences disappeared when differences in motivation were allowed for. The implication was that the learning mechanism was essentially the same at all ages, though it was recognized that there would be changes in learning abilities in relation to the development and decline of sensory powers. On the whole, however, differences in the learning abilities of subjects of different ages reported by experimentalists tended until more recent times to be ascribed to motivational changes occurring in the course of the life cycle. (2) Only in the 1940s and 50s did other developmental changes in learning behaviour begin to be considered and investigated experimentally.

Hebb (3) believed that later learning builds upon, rather than replaces, initial learning; and this in itself would make the characteristics of the two different. He believed that much early learning tended to be permanent. While early learning has been shown, at least in the higher mammals, to be very slow, it could nevertheless be foundational both in furnishing the organism with essential perceptual and motor skills and in providing the basis for subsequent transfer of learning. And Hebb expressed the view that 'the learning of the mature animal owes its efficiency to the slow and inefficient learning that has gone before, but may also be limited and canalized by it' (op cit., p. 109).

More recently, research findings have tended to qualify and specify statements of this kind, rather than confirm or refute them. Various learning capabilities of young subjects and mature subjects have been compared and differences have been reported and evaluated; but the interpretation of such differences has not been easy. Many studies confirmed Hebb's view that restriction of the range of initial experiences tends to affect adversely much later learning; and some of these studies will be considered in Chapter 5. One important outcome of the progress in developmental studies of learning has been the view that the concept of learning, as an entity, may be too general and too crude to allow an adequate investigation of changes of learning capacity with age. (4)

Vince, who arrived at this conclusion, studied and analysed the learning of young and adult passerine birds: chaffinches, titmice, greenfinches and canaries. She trained them in tasks involving the pulling of strings, the lifting of lids, and so on. She considered two features of the learning process: the acquisition, when reinforced, of the appropriate response, and the suppression of the tendency to continue to respond in the absence of reinforcement. Vince found juveniles to be more generally responsive, and capable of acquiring the correct responses more quickly, than mature birds. The latter were, however, found to be better able to inhibit incorrect responses, i.e. to learn not to respond inappropriately. Either the young or the adults could learn more quickly, depending on the character of the task. What is important is not that early learning is less or more efficient than later learning but that early and later learning can differ in certain features. It may, thus, be misleading to adopt any single unitary criterion of learning efficiency.

This view, as Vince points out, is consistent with findings concerning the learning of simple sensory-motor skills by children. Long ago Luria reported studies of children, ranging in age from 2 to 7 years, indicating that young children do not lack in responsiveness; what they do lack is the ability to control their activity, i.e. to suppress unwanted or unhelpful responses. (5) Other students of child development have also drawn attention to developmental changes in learning. Bruner, for instance, following Piaget, emphasizes the role of cognitive growth in children, entailing changes with age of modes of acquiring knowledge. The child's growing understanding of the world may be regarded as model-construction and model-modification. Such models as are being formed are tested against reality only partially and intermittently; and they develop as a function of the uses to which they are being put. (6) Thus the character of model-formation, or knowledge-acquisition, or learning, depends on the level of cognitive development (the level attained in the progression of modes of representation) which in part depends on the nature of the child's experience of interaction with the environment.

A suggestion has been made that what is learned by a young child will not, in many instances, ever be lost, whereas adult learning is essentially rather unstable. The near-irreversibility of childhood learning might occur whenever an association is formed between stimuli of a particular class and a given response before the child is capable of making differentiations within that class. An example is quoted of a child terrorized by his father at a very early stage of development, before the child is capable of discriminating between father and other men. Such a child might react for ever with some fear to all men, or at least to a broad class of men of whom father was initially a member not distinguishable from other members. (7) This is, of course, no more than an interesting suggestion; but it is one of many that emphasizes the differences between early and later learning, and one that may conceivably lead to some fruitful investigations.

III.   *A comparative approach*

The view, or assumption, of the Hebbian tradition is that, irrespective of species, failure to learn early may prevent effective learning later in life. It is also thought that relatively little later learning may greatly consolidate early learning, so that the total effectiveness of the learning experience depends on the conjoinment of the early and late phases. While some early learning is exceptionally durable, some appears to be entirely lost; this differential retention is a remarkable and, presumably, advantageous feature of human learning in infancy.

Some of the traditional aims of comparative psychology, including the comparative psychology of learning, have been criticized in recent years on the ground that learning abilities of different species are essentially not comparable. This renders somewhat unfruitful any attempts at placing species, or even up to a point individuals within a species, on a continuum of learning ability; likewise, attempts at 'equating motivation' of different species in order to make learning comparisons are unlikely to be rewarding. However, sensible inter-species comparisons may be made of the otogeny of learning. The courses of development of learning, the stage sequences, may be studied in various species in the hope of discerning some general developmental lawfulness. For example, are there any general sequences of the so-called critical periods? We shall consider this and related matters later in the book in the light of the available evidence. And we shall adopt, as far as it is feasible, a comparative approach to the ontogeny of learning.

IV   *Modifiability of early behaviour*

Some modes of early behaviour of animals and of human beings are genetically determined; that is, they are automatically evoked by a combination of internal and external stimuli; and such behaviour patterns may or may not be markedly modified through experience. Some other forms of early behaviour emerge very largely as a result of learning, sometimes slow and sometimes rapid. Developmental and comparative psychologists are very much concerned with establishing which of early-behaviour tendencies in various species are substantially fixed and which are readily malleable. There is no short-cut route to these goals, only persistent and painstaking experimental research.

What very young animals and human beings can or cannot learn is only very partially known, and later chapters review this knowledge from one angle and another. To indicate what the investigators in this field are after, we may cite some simple experiments whereby certain initial 'inclinations' of near-neonate animals are first determined, and then the modifiability of such tendencies is investigated to see whether, how far, and by what means the initial behaviour can be altered. Thus, one experiment set out to find out the preferences of day-old domestic-fowl chicks for the 'feel' of different textures; (8) then, the development of attachments to the preferred and the non-preferred textures was investigated. (9) Similarly, shifts in preference for colours were studied as both domestic-fowl and Japanese quail chicks were 'exposure-trained', and also otherwise 'taught' under various conditions and for varying periods of time, to prefer one or another colour. (10, 11) Other related work has been concerned with changes of preference *away* from stimuli to which young chicks had been exposed. (12) Infant guinea-pigs have also been studied in experiments of this type, and some findings are mentioned in later chapters. In investigations of this type a variety of features of early behaviour may be observed under varying conditions, rather than particular types of behaviour only, such as bar-pressing or key-pecking. (13)

The attempts to establish which behaviour tendencies are modifiable, and how far, no more than exemplify certain recent research trends in comparative developmental psychology. The studies of the behaviour of primates at the University of Wisconsin, U.S.A., conducted on a large scale, are essentially directed towards similar ends. In the first place initial inclinations of infant monkeys have been observed; and one of the earliest findings was that very young rhesus monkeys seek 'contact comfort' in clinging to soft surfaces of fur or cloth. (14, 15) The experimental animals have also been exposed to various types of treatment including social isolation, leading to the acquisition of different modes of social behaviour. In particular, young monkeys have been tested for learning abilities and for preference between siblings, mothers and other individuals, after a variety of rearing experiences; (16, 17) but we must defer the consideration of findings of research of this and similar kinds until Chapters 4 and 5. Such research is not confined to animals. Certain studies of human infants may also be thought of as being concerned with the modifiability of early behaviour. Thus Schaffer and colleagues have been investigating proximity-seeking and proximity-avoidance behaviour in human infants, and how these modes of behaviour develop with time; (18, 19) but, again, more about such research – in later chapters.

V. *The study of early learning*

The use of the phrase 'early learning' in psychological literature is not to be taken as implying that early learning is one of the types or classes of learning. From the viewpoint of the experimentalist learning may be observed in a number of distinct situations or conditions, each characterized by certain definable features. In this vein Gagné (20) distinguishes signal learning, stimulus-response learning, chaining, verbal association, and so on. Other such classifications are also, of course, possible. How these different specifiable conditions of learning fit into the various learning theories is a different matter (see Chapter 10). Early learning, like adult learning, may also be considered in terms of the learning conditions, although some of these conditions are more typical of learning in adulthood while others are equally common in infancy. Furthermore, within each condition, early and later learning may follow somewhat different courses; only experimental studies of learning similar tasks at different ages can throw more light on this.

In studying the learning of any individual, young or otherwise, one may be interested in learning capacity, in the rate of learning, in the generalization or transfer of learning, and in the retention of what has been learned. In studying learning developmentally, in observing changes in the character of learning with age, or in looking for any characteristic features of infantile learning, the investigator is still concerned with the learner's abilities, including his learning speed, in his power to profit indirectly from his experience and in his power to remember what he has 'taken in'. (21) Thus it is not the questions as such which are asked about early learning that are different. What is special about the study of early learning is that the focus of attention is directed towards learning in physically immature individuals, towards learning with a minimum of prior experience, and learning that appears to be foundational. And what may be special about early learning – sometimes unique perhaps – are the findings; for, as will be seen later, while some early learning has not been found to have any distinguishing characteristics, some forms of early learning are especially interesting and, indeed, remarkable.

NOTES

1 T. C. Schneirla, 'The Concept of Development in Comparative Psychology', in *The Concept of Development*, ed. D. B. Harris, 1957, Minneapolis: University of Minnesota Press.

2 B. A. Campbell, 'Developmental Studies of Learning and Motivation in Infra-Primate Mammals', in *Early Behavior*, eds. H. W. Stevenson, E. H. Hess and H. L. Rheingold, 1967, New York: Wiley.

3 D. O. Hebb, *The Organization of Behavior: a Neuropsychological Theory*, 1949, New York: Wiley.

4. M. A. Vince, 'Developmental Changes in Learning Capacity', in *Current Problems in Animal Behaviour*, eds. W. H. Thorpe and O. L. Zangwill, 1961, Cambridge: Cambridge University Press.

5 A. R. Luria, *The Nature of Human Conflicts*, 1932, New York: Liveright

6 J. S. Bruner, R. R. Olver and P. M. Greenfield, *Studies in Cognitive Growth*, 1966, New York: Wiley.

7 K. J. Rohde, 'Effect of Early Experience on the Child: Possible Solution to Controversy', *Psychol. Rep.*, 1967, *20*, p. 134.

8 W. Sluckin, K. F. Taylor and Ann Taylor, 'Approach of Domestic Chicks to Stationary Objects of Different Texture', *Percept. Mot. Skills*, 1966, *22*, pp. 699–702.

9 Ann Taylor, W. Sluckin, Rosemary Hewitt and P. Guiton, 'The Formation of Attachments by Domestic Chicks to Two Textures', *Anim. Behav.*, 1967, *15*, pp. 512–517.

10 Ann Taylor, W. Sluckin and Rosemary Hewitt, 'Changing Colour Preference of Chicks', *Anim. Behav.*, 1969, *17*, pp. 3–8.

11 Ann Taylor and W. Sluckin, 'Shifts of Colour Preference in Day-old Chicks after Training and Delay, *Percept. Mot. Skills*, 1968, *27*, pp. 955–958.

12 M. Herbert and W. Sluckin, 'Acquisition of Colour Preferences by Chicks at Different Temperatures', *Anim. Behav.*, 1969, *17*, pp. 213–216.

13 P. Guiton and W. Sluckin, 'The Effects of Visual Experience on Behavioural Development in Neonatal Domestic Chicks', *Br. J. Psychol.*, 1969, *60*, pp. 495–507.

14 H. F. Harlow and R. R. Zimmermann, 'Affectional Responses in the Infant Monkey', *Science*, 1959, *130*, pp. 421–432.

15 H. F. Harlow, 'The Development of Affectional Patterns in Infant Monkeys', in *Determinants of Infant Behaviour, I.*, ed. B. M. Foss, 1961, London: Methuen.

16 H. F. Harlow, 'Total Social Isolation: Effects on Macaque Monkey Behaviour', *Science*, 1965, *148*, p. 666.

17 G. P. Sackett, G. A. Griffin, C. Pratt, W. D. Joslyn and G. Ruppenthal, 'Mother-infant and Adult Female Choice Behaviour in Rhesus Monkeys after Various Rearing Experiences', *J. Comp. Physiol. Psychol*, 1967, *63*, pp. 376–381.

18 H. R. Schaffer and P. E. Emerson, 'Patterns of Response to Physical Contact in Early Human Development', *J. Child Psychol. Psychiat*, 1964, *5*, pp. 1–13.

19 H. R. Schaffer, 'The Onset of Fear of Strangers and the Incongruity Hypothesis', *J. Child Psychol. Psychiat.*, 1966, *7*, pp. 95–106.

20 R. M. Gagné, *The Conditions of Learning*, 1967, New York: Holt Rinehart and Winston.

21 R. R. Zimmermann and C. C. Torrey, 'Ontogeny of Learning', in *Behavior of Nonhuman Primates; Vol. II.*, eds. A. M. Schrier, H. F. Harlow and F. Stollnitz, 1965, New York: Academic Press.

CHAPTER 2

Conditioning the Young

The term 'conditioning' is not a precise one. Originally it meant training animals in the manner devised by Pavlov. Later the term also began to be used for somewhat different methods of training. At the same time theorists were asking to what extent seemingly complex learning might be explained in terms of relatively simple conditioning. As a result, the word 'conditioning' often with a qualifying adjective, has come to refer also to a basic learning process thought to occur within the organism rather than just a training procedure adopted by the experimenter. The assumption has been that much, if not all, human learning could be analysed into, and understood in terms of, such basic forms of learning.

For our present purpose we may ignore the theoretical overtones of the term 'conditioning'. Therefore, conditioning can be regarded as signifying a range of experimental procedures used traditionally for bringing about certain kinds of behavioural change in animals and human beings. One of them is, of course, Pavlovian or classical conditioning, for which also certain other labels have been used, e.g. respondent conditioning, signal learning, etc. Some experimental procedures fall quite clearly into this category, while others do so with less certainty.

A variety of other conditioning procedures have been used, and they have been sometimes lumped together under some common name such as instrumental conditioning. From the point of view of the methods of training used in experimental studies, it is convenient to list several non-classical types of conditioning procedures. One is 'reward training' – an almost self-explanatory term. Another is escape conditioning in which the experimental subject learns to escape from a painful situation. Yet another type is avoidance conditioning whereby the subject learns to act in some way which prevents a painful experience. These are only some of the types of conditioning procedure that have been used; and a variety of classifications are possible. In this chapter we simply propose to survey the various experimental methods and findings that have accumulated from the study of conditioning in very young animal and human subjects.

I. Chicks, puppies and other infant animals

Continuing in the footsteps of Pavlov, many Russian research workers have been investigating the conditionability of very young animals, and notably dogs. Some years ago, Kliavina *et al* (1) listed a sizeable bibliography on the conditioning of puppies, and also reported some further findings of their own, arguing against the earlier view that young puppies could not be as readily conditioned as the more mature animals. A little earlier, J. P. Scott, (2) reporting previous work, concluded that no stable conditioning of puppies was possible before the age of about 20 days. There were also strong indications that this early period of the dog's life was one during which no socialization was possible. Yet some years later other American workers, (3) using a puff of air as the conditioned stimulus and shock as the unconditioned one, obtained clear-cut evidence of the ability of puppies well under three weeks of age to acquire aversive conditioned responses. More recently, other workers reported aversive conditioning in even younger puppies; and food-reinforced conditioning has been established in puppies only days old. (4)

It is known that the myelination of the brain of young puppies is very incomplete. It may be that the initial limited conditionability of infant animals is related to this, and that improvement in conditionability depends on the progress of myelination. But it is still an open question as to whether the staged improvement with age of the reliability and accuracy of the conditioned response reported in puppies (3) is due mainly to the maturation of the central nervous system, or primarily to the gradually accruing conditioning experience.

The conditionability of newborn rats, up to 24 hours old, was investigated in one study, using a vibro-tactile conditioned stimulus repeatedly paired with an electric shock administered to the animal's forelimb; by this means some limited degree of conditioning was successfully brought about. (5) In another study, groups of neonates were reared under different learning conditions up to the third day after birth. Rats kept in an incubator and tube-fed were found after a number of forced-feeding trials to respond to stimuli associated with food injection in a markedly different way (by wriggling, squealing and suckling) from infant rats reared by their mothers. (6) Thus, provided appropriate conditioning opportunities are created, neonatal rats will show some learning capacity.

The study of learning in weanling rats presents rather fewer technical difficulties; and some research effort has been devoted over a period of years to that stage of development. (7) The initial problem to be faced was that of equating, as far as possible, the motivational states of the young and mature animals, so that any variations in performance at different ages could be assigned to differences in learning ability as distinct from motivational differences. Equating deprivation of food and water certainly does not equate motivation, for there is evidence that the strength of deprivation-produced drives depends greatly on the age of the animal. However, electric shock appears to provide relatively uniform motivating conditions in similar animals of different ages. In fact, Campbell and co-workers, (7) having first demonstrated that there were no developmental differences of much consequence in the sensitivity of rats to low intensities of electric shock, then used electric shock as the reinforcing agent in a series of conditioning studies. Comparisons were made between juvenile and adult rats in their ability to learn to escape from an area of electric shock, but little difference, if at all, was found between the two groups. The young animals tended to forget what they had learned more quickly than the adults. Likewise, juveniles were found to be as good as adults at avoidance learning, but not as good at retaining what had been learned. No evidence was found that fear responses acquired early in life were more durable than those acquired later. On the contrary, the effects of fearful experiences were found to fade quite quickly in young rats. So much for the suggestion, as far as rats are concerned, that early learning is persistent or irreversible.

Rats, like dogs, are altricial animals; and they are entirely incapable in their earliest infancy of the kind of learning just considered. However, guinea-pigs, which have also been studied developmentally, are capable of locomotion soon after birth and, therefore, it might be expected, of escape learning. It has been reported that guinea-pigs just under two days of age are, if anything, better than adults at escape learning, but – like juvenile rats – tend to forget what they have learned rather quickly. (7) Other precocial mammals studied were lambs and kids. The youngest could be conditioned as early as four hours after birth in a situation in which a mild electric shock to the leg was used as the unconditioned stimulus and a sudden dimming of lights as the conditioned stimulus to which the animals learned to respond with leg flexion. (8)

Volokhov lists the times of the first appearance and of the consolidation of the conditioned defence reflex to sound in various animals during their ontogenetic development. (9) Such responses begin to be acquired on the day of birth by the guinea-pig, at 7–11 days by the rabbit, at 10–15 days by the rat, at 17–25 days by the dog, and at 22–28 days by the cat. The review also surveys Russian studies of the formation of other types of conditioned response, mainly in the dog. Among bird species, the pigeon is specifically mentioned.

The pigeon hatches out in a quite immature state. On the other hand, the domestic-fowl chick is a precocial animal, and probably for this reason its conditionability has been studied at a very early age. Day-old chicks move readily from a cold to a warm environment, but cannot be conditioned to avoid the latter when it is associated with painful stimulation. Escape from, or avoidance of, electric shock may first be learned on the third day of life. (10, 11, 12) At any rate, avoidance learning may readily be brought about in most chicks at four days, and invariably in one-week-old subjects. (13)

II.   *Young monkeys*

Something is known about the conditionability of young subhuman primates, especially – the rhesus monkey. Conditioning studies, using infant monkeys as subjects, have been conducted at the Primate Research Center of the University of Wisconsin. In one of them infants ranging from 2 to 14 days of age were classically conditioned, receiving a number of daily pairings of shock (unconditioned stimulus) and tone (conditioned stimulus). (14) On test the tone stimulus was presented alone, and strong evidence of conditioning (increased overt activity, both observed and recorded) was found. In another study monkeys only one day old were trained: a 1000-cps tone was repeatedly coupled with electric shock delivered through the floor-grid, and tone-only presentations were given on test. (15) It was found that the young animals quite soon learned to respond to the tone alone with leaping, hopping, crouching or immobility.

It appears that, depending on the physical maturity of the particular organism, monkeys shortly after birth are susceptible to classical conditioning and can learn instrumentally a range of locomotory and manipulatory responses. Rather older monkeys have been reported to be capable of learning to respond to a signal by approaching a feeding booth. At 2 or 3 weeks manipulatory activity is in evidence, both in consequence of being rewarded with food, and, to some extent, as an end in itself. (16)

Within one month of birth monkeys appear to be capable of learning colour and pattern discriminations and may even learn discrimination reversals. Learning to delay responses and acquiring 'learning sets' comes several months after birth. Even very intensive training of young animals on such problems does not bring about learning which is anything like as efficient as that of adults. And more recent work, while confirming that instrumental learning with noxious reinforcement develops rapidly in the newborn rhesus monkey, indicates that the ability to acquire conditioned emotional behaviour makes its appearance in ontogeny only quite slowly. (17)

Generally, adult monkeys are able to learn a great deal more than infants. Whatever infants can be taught, adults can learn more rapidly; and adults probably also retain longer what they have learned, although findings concerning memory at different ages are scanty. Leaving human beings aside, it may be said that in primates some learning abilities are present very early in life; and further important learning powers develop only gradually. Whether certain learning abilities improve at some early stage and then decline is uncertain; that is, it is not clear whether there is any early period which could be described as the sensitive period for some types of learning. On the whole, however, students of learning in non-human primates have not set out to search for any such sensitive periods, including the possible critical periods for socialization. We shall return to this problem in Chapter 6, when we will be specifically concerned with sensitive periods in the development of behaviour.

III.   *Human infants*

The conditionability of human infants has been fairly extensively studied since the second decade of this century. Classical conditioning procedures have been used a great deal, and a comprehensive review of the earlier Russian work is provided by Kasatkin. (18) Many studies have used milk as the reinforcing agent, but non-nutritive sucking has also been found to provide reinforcement. Earlier reports indicated that classical conditioning was impossible or very difficult to attain in very young infants; and no stable conditioning had been reliably reported before the age of 10 days. (19, 20) As techniques have continued to improve, the earlier general conclusion has had to be revised. In one study, for instance, the pairing of a low-frequency loud tone with the insertion of a nipple in a baby's mouth resulted in conditioned responses to the sound alone in the infant's third or fourth day of life. (20, 21) In other experiments conditioned head-turning in infants from 1 to 4 days of age was established by strengthening the head-turning response through various reinforcement contingencies. (22) Using dextrose-water solution, there was an increase in the occurrence of the reinforced response and a habituation of the non-reinforced one.

Aversive conditioning, which may be regarded as being largely in the classical-conditioning tradition, has also been studied quite extensively. The unconditioned aversive stimuli used have been mainly light electric shock, loud sounds, and puffs of air directed to the infant's eye; and various visual and auditory conditioned stimuli have been coupled with them. In an early well-known study, a shock to the sole of the foot was paired with a buzzer sound, the subjects being under-ten-day-old infants. Conditioning to buzzer was seemingly achieved in the experimental group; but a similar response to the buzzer occurred also in the control group members of which had received shocks without the buzzer sound. (23) Since members of another control group tested repeatedly for responses to the buzzer without any shock tended not to respond like the subjects in the first two groups, it was concluded that, while modification of behaviour, or some form of learning, did result from the shock experience, there was doubt as to whether any specific conditioning took place. In fact, the interpretation of the results of this study was subsequently a subject of some debate, which emphasized the need for much stricter controls in experimentation of this kind.

Lipsitt has reported in detail both on earlier studies and on research work conducted by himself and his collaborators. (20) While aversive conditioning in infants some months old is possible, attempts to condition aversive reactions in neonates had earlier produced uncertain results. (24) Perhaps it would be rash to assume that further improvements in technique will not make it possible to achieve stable aversive conditioning of newborn infants; for, as mentioned earlier, such improvements have recently permitted some operant conditioning of very young babies. As matters stood some years ago, it seemed reasonable to conclude that really rapid conditioning to visual stimulation was first possible at about ten weeks of age, and to auditory stimulation probably rather earlier. Until quite recently research findings tended to indicate that conditioning of infants under ten days of age, if achieved, was unstable, (25) but it now looks as if present-day research will necessitate a revision of this generalization.

In neonates the distinction between respondent and operant behaviour is somewhat blurred, (22) and therefore conditioning procedures do not always lend themselves to ready labelling. This is much less so in the case of older infants. Conditioning studies of such infants, around the age of six months or thereabouts, using instrumental procedures, were first attempted more than half a century ago (26) and have continued since. Sweet substances have mostly been used as rewards but other kinds of reinforcement, such as picking up the baby, smiling at it, etc., have also been made use of to bring about discriminative learning. Babies have been found to be capable of learning discriminations between colours, positions, and so on. Some early work has suggested that much operant conditioning could occur in infants several days old. And some writers believe that this mode of learning is of crucial importance in early infancy. (27) This might be so, but such a view is in present circumstances entirely open to debate. Further research should make it possible to base pronouncements in this field on more firmly empirical foundations.

Perhaps the importance of the study of conditioning in the earliest infancy, when it is achieved in the laboratory only with difficulty, should not be exaggerated. At any rate, a much greater range of learning is possible at some months, rather than days, of age. Developmental studies aim at tracing the ontogeny of condition-ability. Valuable studies are conducted on a number of fronts. One interesting area of study is that of conditioned orienting responses. It is remarkable that the most effective reinforcers for such learning have been found to be new and changing stimuli rather than conventional rewards. (28, 29) The acquisition of discriminative behaviour is another important area of research. Some workers have found evidence of this learning ability in the first few days of life. (22) How stable is such training, and indeed any learning during the first days and weeks of life, is not altogether clear. This is one of the problems of developmental psychology where a great deal of research is needed. Nevertheless it is clear that newly born human infants *can learn* some responses under certain specific conditions. (30) How much they actually *do learn* in every-day life is another matter. Some developmental and personality theories make various assumptions about the role of the earliest learning in shaping later behaviour. The present state of knowledge does not allow much more than speculation on such matters.

IV. *Some concluding remarks*

We may now attempt some tentative generalizations about early conditioning in anmals and man. Clearly it is very difficult to say when a given form of conditioning is first possible; for a great deal depends on the ingenuity and determination of the investigator. As better experimental mehods become available, conditioning is achieved in ever younger individuals. Other things being equal, in species in which the young are born at relatively advanced levels of development, conditioning is possible sooner after birth than in less precocial species. Human infants do not appear to be more susceptible to conditioning than infant animals at comparable stages of physical development. On the whole it is impossible to be sure at the present time that either in animals or in human beings any one form of conditioning will consistently succeed before any other. Lastly, it looks as if the earliest conditioning is slow, and the evidence about its tenacity is still uncertain. In this respect early conditioning contrasts with early imprinting; for the latter – to which we must now turn – is in some cases at least both quite quick and relatively durable.

NOTES

1 M. P. Kliavina, E. M. Kobakova, L. N. Stel'makh and V. A. Troshikhin, 'Speed of Formation of Conditional Reflexes in Dogs in the Course of Ontogenesis', *Zh. Vyssh. Nerv. Deiatel.*, 1958, *8*, pp. 929–936.

2 J. P. Scott, 'The Genetic and Environmental Differentiation in Behavior', in *The Concept of Development*, ed. D. B. Harris, 1957, Minneapolis: University of Minnesota Press.

3 A. C. Cornwell and J. L. Fuller, 'Conditioned Responses in Young Puppies', *J. Comp. Physiol. Psychol.*, 1961, *54, pp.* 13–15.

4 W. C. Stanley, A. C. Cornwell, C. Poggiani and A. Trattner, 'Conditioning in the Neonatal Puppy', *J. Comp. Physiol. Psychol.*, 1963, *56*, pp. 211–214.

5 D. F. Caldwell and J. Werboff, 'Classical Conditioning in Newborn Rats', *Science*, 1962, *136*, pp. 1118–1119.

6 E. Thoman, A. Wetzel and S. Levine, 'Learning in the Neonatal Rat', *Anim. Behav.*, 1968, *16*, pp. 54–57.

7 B. A. Campbell, 'Developmental Studies of Learning and Motivation in Infra-primate Mammals', in *Early Behavior*, eds. H. W. Stevenson, E. H. Hess and H. L. Rheingold, 1967, New York: Wiley.

8 A. U. Moore, 'Conditioning and Stress in the Newborn Lamb and Kid', in *Physiological Bases of Psychiatry*, ed. W. H. Gantt, 1958, Springfield, Ill.: C. C. Thomas.

9 A. A. Volokhov, 'A Comparative Physiological Study of Uncon-

ditioned and Conditioned Reflexes in the Course of Ontogenesis', *Zh. Vyssh. Nerv. Deiatel.*, 1959, *9*, pp. 52–62.

10 J. J. Peters and R. L. Isaacson, 'Acquisition of Active and Passive Responses in two Breeds of Chickens', *J. Comp. Physiol. Psychol.*, 1963, *56*, pp. 793–796.

11 H. James and C. Binks, 'Escape and Avoidance Learning in Newly Hatched Domestic Chicks', *Science*, 1963, *139*, pp. 1293–1294.

12 R. K. Siegel, 'Avoidance Learning in the Neonate Chick', *Psychol. Rep.*, 1967, *21*, pp. 809–812.

13 G. J. Fischer and G. L. Campbell, 'The Development of Passive Avoidance Conditioning in Leghorn Chicks', *Anim. Behav.*, 1964, *12*, pp. 268–269.

14 W. A. Mason and H. F. Harlow, 'Formation of Conditioned Responses in Infant Monkeys', *J. Comp. Physiol. Psychol.*, 1958, *51*, pp. 68–70.

15 P. C. Green, 'Learning, Extinction and Generalization of Conditioned Responses by Young Monkeys', *Psychol. Rep.*, 1962, *10*, pp. 731–738.

16 R. R. Zimmermann and C. C. Torrey, 'Ontogeny of Learning', in *Behavior of Nonhuman Primates, Vol. II*, eds. A. M. Schrier, H. F. Harlow and F. Stollnitz, 1965, New York: Academic Press.

17 G. W. Meier and C. Garcia-Rodriguez, 'Development of Conditional Behaviors in the Infant Rhesus Monkey', *Psychol. Rep.*, 1966, *19*, pp. 1159–1169.

18 N. I. Kasatkin, 'Early Ontogenesis of Reflex Activity in the Child', *Zh. Vyssh. Nerv. Deiatel.*, 1957, 7, pp. 805–818.

19 R. W. Kantrow, 'An Investigation of Conditioned Feeding Responses and Concomitant Adaptive Behavior in Young Infants', *Univ. Iowa Stud. Child Welf.*, 1937, *13(3)*, pp. 1–64.

20 L. P. Lipsitt, 'Learning in the First Year of Life', in *Advances in Child Development and Behavior*, eds. L. P. Lipsitt and C. C. Spiker, 1963, New York: Acadamic Press.

21 L. P. Lipsitt and H. Kaye, 'Conditioned Sucking in the Human Newborn', *Psychon. Sci.*, 1964, *1*, pp. 29–30.

22 E. R. Siqueland and L. P. Lipsitt, 'Conditioned Head-turning in Human Newborns', *J. Exp. Child Psychol.*, 1966, *3*, pp. 356–376.

23 D. D. Wickens and C. Wickens, 'A Study of Conditioning in the Neonate', *J. Exp. Psychol.*, 1940, *26*, pp. 94–102.

24 M. A. Wenger, 'An Investigation of Conditioned Responses in Infants', *Univ. Iowa Stud. Child Welf.*, 1936, *12(1)*, pp. 9–90.

25 J. P. Scott, 'The Process of Primary Socialization in Canine and Human Infants', *Monogr. Soc. Res. Child Development*, 1963, *28(1)*, pp. 1–47.

26 C. W. Valentine, 'The Colour Perception and Colour Preferences

of an Infant during its Fourth and Eighth Months, *Br. J. Psychol.*, 1914, *6*, pp. 363–386.

27 S. W. Bijou and D. M. Baer, *Child Development*, Vol. II, 1965, New York: Appleton-Century-Crofts.

28 J. Koch, 'Conditioned Orienting Reactions in Two-month-old Infants', *Br. J. Psychol.*, 1967, *58*, pp. 105–110.

29 J. Koch, 'Conditioned Orienting Reactions to Persons and Things in 2–5-month-old Infants', *Human Devel.*, 1968, *11*, pp. 81–91.

30 L. P. Lipsitt, 'Can Human Newborns Learn?' *Bull. Br. Psychol. Soc.*, 1966, *19* (No. 65), pp. 71–72.

CHAPTER 3

Classical Imprinting

The type of early learning, which is known as imprinting, was initially observed and studied in precocial birds. Although this behaviour had been reported and described earlier, it was Konrad Lorenz who named it and who drew special attention to it. (1, 2) Lorenz's original claims, that imprinting is irreversible and that it is narrowly confined to a short sensitive period, have not, on the whole, been borne out by subsequent investigations. (3, 4) However, the impetus given to research into imprinting by Lorenz's writings has been powerful. Studies of imprinting have proliferated, and a number of reviews and evaluations of the research have now appeared. (5, 6) Although the term, imprinting, has more recently been used with reference to some ways of learning by adults as well as by neonates, and of learning in mammals as well as in birds, what may be called classical imprinting is concerned with the acquisition of more-or-less specific attachments by young precocial birds without the mediation of conventional rewards such as food or water.

I. *The initial stages*

The young of the avian species, described as nidifugous, are capable of locomotion soon after hatching. They tend to approach some features of their environments and to follow anything moving. The tendency to follow moving figures used to be regarded as central to imprinting. It is now known that young birds can form attachments irrespective of following behaviour. (7, 8) Nevertheless in most investigations of classical imprinting, approach and following responses have been at the inception of imprinting.

Stimuli vary, of course, in their effectiveness in eliciting approach or following. As might be expected, visual and auditory stimuli combined are more effective in evoking approach than either mode of stimulation alone. (9) It is well established that young chicks, ducklings, and the like, reared in isolation, retain their propensity to approach and follow any salient figures very much longer than those reared in groups. This is so most probably because socially reared animals become imprinted to one another and consequently recognize and shun strange figures, whereas singly reared animals (especially if kept in visually monotonous environments) continue to be attracted by new prominent and not-too-intense stimuli. (3, 10, 11)

II. *The testing of imprinting*

Sooner or later the fledgelings will form some imprinted attachments. How are we to judge that imprinting has occurred? Several criteria may be used. First, experimental animals will tend to make 'distress' calls when separated from the figure to which they have become attached, whereas control animals that have not been long enough in the proximity of the figure will tend not to make such calls when separated from it. This may be described as the *distress-at-separation test*. Second, animals 'exposure-trained' with a figure, and then reconfronted with it at a later and less sensitive stage of development, will tend – if imprinting has taken place – to approach and follow it more readily than control animals reared in similar conditions but without the requisite experience. This we may call the *recognition-at-reunion test*. Third, imprinted animals will tend to choose the familiar figure in a discrimination test, whereas control animals will continue to show no preference as between initially equally attractive figures. (12) We may call this the *choice test*. Fourth, imprinted animals with a familiar figure, when not close to it, will approach it and stay with it whenever confronted with a strange figure. We may describe this procedural variant of the previous situation as the *'run-to-mother' test*. Fifth, imprinted animals will tend to work in an operant set-up in order to gain the sight of, or access to, the familiar figure, while unimprinted post-sensitive-period animals will behave as if the figure were not such a worthwhile end to be gained. (13) We may call this the *work-for-reunion test*. In addition to these relatively short-term criteria, a long-term sign of imprinting is the tendency in imprinted males to court, at maturity, figures similar to those with which they have become familiar; but more will be said about such sexual imprinting in a later section.

III. *Effectiveness of stimulus figures*

Some stimulus figures are initially more attractive than others. These attractive figures need not, in theory, be of necessity best for imprinting purposes; in practice, however, figures which readily elicit aproach seem the most suitable for imprinting. In one study, 'striking' patterned models were found to have been preferred not only by 'naïve' domestic chicks, but also by those that had been trained for a relatively short time with a plain white object. (14) Evidently a great deal of training with an initially unattractive or non-preferred figure is needed if such training is to offset the 'built-in' predilictions for certain colours and patterns. Experiments with domestic ducklings have also indicated that 'the effects of imprinting procedure vary with the stimuli presented'. (15)

IV. *Imprinting with static environment*

The characteristics of stimulus figures have a bearing on the development of attachments by infant animals not only in the context of typical imprinting to moving figures but also when imprinting takes place in relation to the various features of the animals' stationary environment. It is known that birds tend to have preferences for certain colours over others, both in terms of pecking and of approach responses. It has also been found that approach preferences of chicks for colours can be modified in a variety of ways, and quite effectively by exposing the animals for some hours, or even minutes, to the coloured walls of their pens. It has been established that exposure to a non-preferred colour can be markedly effective in bringing about a shift of preference towards it. (16) Like-wise, exposure of chicks to non-preferred tactile stimulation can shift the animals' preference in the direction of the initially non-preferred texture. (17)

V. *Familiarity and fear*

Exposure to any given stimuli results in familiarity with these stimuli. This shows itself in the animal's ability to discriminate between the familiar and the strange, the former being sought and the latter avoided. Aversive or withdrawal behaviour, or fear, may thus be the consequence of exposure learning which underlies the development of imprinting attachments. This view is consistent with Hebb's incongruity hypothesis of fear. (18, 19) It is, of course, possible to implant fear in an animal through conditioning to painful stimuli. And fear may be the unconditioned response to certain types of stimulation – for example, when the retinal image increases at a fast rate as the subject faces a 'looming' stimulus. However, it is clear that some fear responses are entailed by the imprinting process itself. (12, 20)

It might be thought that newly hatched nidifugous birds, being without prior visual stimulation, will be fearless when confronted with any salient features in their new environment. While it is true that such chicks, as soon as mobile, tend to respond to salient stimuli with approach and following, none-the-less naïve chicks have been observed on occasions to show withdrawal responses to stimuli which cannot readily be described as particularly intense. Of course, their intensity should probably be considered in terms of contrast between previous and current experience, rather than in any absolute terms; and any marked contrast would then account for the fear-evoking quality of some stimuli presented to birds immediately after their emergence from the egg-shell or from the dark in which they have been kept after hatching. On the whole, however, dark-raised animals show little fear, and such few signs as may be observed are generally a response to the so-called looming visual stimulation mentioned earlier. (21)

While animals with no prior visual experience generally show no fear of relatively weak stimuli, animals with experience of complex stimulation are also relatively fearless of the strange. The latter is the result of habituation, or extinction of the animals' reactivity. Thus, there appears to be an inverted-U relationship between fear and prior visual experience, whereby fear of novelty rises to a maximum and then declines as the complexity of earlier visual experience increases. (22) However, the exact nature of this relationship remains yet to be more fully investigated experimentally.

VI.   *Sexual imprinting*

Doubts have been raised from time to time as to whether specific imprinted attachments which show themselves as exposure-acquired preferences are continuous with sexual imprinting. Some investigators maintain that the relatively short-term approach preferences are acquired a little earlier than the relatively longer-term courtship preferences. (23, 24) Much evidence from 'field' observations, and some from quantitative laboratory investigations, has been reviewed to show that sexual imprinting of varying degrees is widespread. (5, 6) Some students of imprinting continue to hold the view implicit in the earlier notion of imprinting, namely that the direction which sexual behaviour takes is an integral feature of the imprinting process. One study of male turkeys, some of which had been imprinted to turkeys and others to human beings, suggests strongly that imprinting should be regarded as a preferential rather than exclusive response – social or sexual. (25) Social attachments, known as tameness when directed to the human species, appear to be the condition for courtship preferences. While attachment shows itself in selective proximity seeking, it may also entail aggressive pecking; furthermore, at an appropriate developmental stage, an imprinted attachment may manifest itself in sexual responses. (26, 27, 28) More research will be needed to determine to what extent approach-and-following imprinting and sexual imprinting are separate phenomena.

A special form of sexual imprinting has been extensively studied in ducks, namely their homosexual behaviour. This can be brought about in males by rearing them together for about 3 months, but not in females whose sexual responses do not appear to be susceptible to redirection. (29) Schutz, working in a field-station in Bavaria, found that such mutual homosexual attachments of drakes are remarkably durable. Males court each other in the normal manner, and the fact that copulation is not achieved does not disrupt the bond which persists for many years. Unlike other manifestations of sexual imprinting which are preferential, this type of homosexuality appears to be exclusive.

VII. *Altricial birds*

Thus far we have been concerned with imprinting in nidifugous birds. If imprinting were thought of as being built upon approach and following responses, then it would be confined to such precocial species only. However, attachments – including sexual imprinting – have been shown to be essentially exposure-acquired, even if they often are greatly facilitated by approach and following. Thus, imprinting in the broader sense could also occur in altricial species, i.e. those species in which the newly hatched young are initially immobile and otherwise helpless. Such young are not only unable to follow moving figures, but may also, while in the nest, begin to be learning which stimuli are associated wth the reward of food. Nevertheless, research findings indicate that sexual preferences, and even fixations, may be basically exposure-acquired by various altricial species of birds.

Such learning, essentially imprinting-like in character, has been known to exist for a long time. Pigeons were the subjects of early observations. (30) Later, signs of sexual imprinting were reported in passerine birds, in birds of prey, in the crow family, and in species of other genera. However, most work has been done on columbiformes, i.e. pigeon and dove species; and the full list of studies is not yet a very long one. (31) Furthermore, many of the reports merely suggest the possibility of sexual imprinting. This is not surprising in view of the practical difficultes of studying imprinting in altricial species: the long time it takes for such birds to attain mobility and later to reach the courtship stage, the space needed for such experimentation, the complexities inherent in the testing of experimental and control subjects, and generally – the difficulty of separating imprinting from instrumental learning in altricial species.

The most thorough experimental studies of imprinting in a

number of dove species have been conducted by Klinghammer. (31, 32) It is clear that young ring-doves, if raised individually by people, can become attached to them and will later prefer people as objects of courtship. Not only the experiences up to the fledgeling stage, but also the subsequent ones, influence the choice of sexual partner. Likewise, mourning-doves will select human beings as mates if exposed to them at the appropriate sensitive period; this preference gradually wanes and after a number of years human beings are no longer preferable to their own species. All this applies essentially to both males and females of the species.

It should be noted that in the case of precocial birds imprinting refers both to the method of training (i.e. exposure-training rather than reinforcement-training) as well as to the consequential attachments which may be assessed by the recognized criteria listed earlier. In altricial birds, the animals' tameness brought about by hand-rearing cannot be ascribed solely to imprinting because existing experimental studies have not attempted to separate exposure to people from hand-rearing. However, the tendency to court people must surely be regarded as imprinted in that, while food-seeking approach responses may have been rewarded, sexual responses will not have actually occurred during the 'training' phase. A sexual preference for the given figure is preceded by tameness towards that figure, however achieved; and such sexual preference, not being the result of 'appropriate' training, would appear to be tied to the acquired familiarity with the given figure or type of figure.

VIII. *Some research trends*

Classical imprinting situations are those in which a newly hatched nidifugous bird develops an attachment to a salient visual pattern such as a moving figure. Responses to auditory stimulation have also been quite extensively studied; but attachments to different auditory patterns have been investigated very little. A number of workers have tried to find out whether anything which could be described as auditory imprinting occurs in newly hatched birds, such as domestic ducklings and chicks. It is known that in many species the young 'recognize' and respond to maternal calls. It is now clear that, in some species at least, they do this in the absence of any prior learning, associative or exposure-acquired. (33) Whether the attractiveness of maternal calling, such as quacking or clucking, is normally independent of experience, whether it can be enhanced through early learning, and whether auditory imprinting occurs in any species, are matters for further research.

Now auditory stimuli have been used a great deal in conjunction with visual imprinting. Such stimuli attract the attention of the subject to the visual patterns with which the young animal eventually becomes imprinted; auditory stimulation then has – it is said – an arousal value. (34) These sounds, however, do not typically appear to generate any development of auditory attachments. This does not, of course, mean that auditory imprinting is, in principle, impossible, for it yet remains to be seen whether 'self-reinforced' differential attachments can develop under more favourable conditions. In order to investigate this, auditory isolation of experimental subjects from unwanted sounds, as well as appropriate means of differential auditory stimulation, would have to be maintained. When these facilities become more readily available new light is likely to be shed on this problem.

A study suggesting that a form of auditory imprinting of young domestic-fowl chicks might be possible has involved exposing eggs at 12–18 days of incubation to specific sounds. (35) The particular tone used proved more effective in evoking approach responses in 'experimental' chicks than another tone when the experimental subjects were tested within six hours of hatching; the same two tones were not differentially attractive to control chicks similarly tested for preference. Exposing incubating eggs to stimulation by sound or by light is a promising line of research. Whether experience of the embryo, auditory or visual, can result in behaviour modifications which have anything in common with imprinting is another matter. So far it has been established that young domestic chicks hatched from eggs incubated in darkness are more ready to make approach and following responses, or show less fear, than similar chicks hatched from eggs incubated in illumination. (36) Experimental procedures of this type may prove important for the study of the development of perception and reactivity in young animals.

IX.   *The character of imprinting*

Lorenz originally regarded imprinting as a phenomenon quite different from known learning processes, but later inclined to the view that imprinting was a form of conditioning. Hess insisted for quite a long time that the differences between imprinting and association learning were of a fundamental nature. (37) On the other hand, Hinde repeatedly expressed the view that such differences had more to do with the varying situations in which learning occurred than with any basic discontinuity between imprinting and other forms of learning. (38) As it is, the various, supposedly unique features of imprinting have turned out – in the light of fast accumulating experimental evidence – to be rather elusive, if not illusory. And views such as those exemplified by the suggestion that imprinting might simply be 'conditioning of an innate social response to a specific stimulus' have been expressed. (39) At this level of discourse there is much scope for debate.

There are, however, other types of approach to the problem. One suggests that imprintng may be thought of as an occurrence whereby 'repeated stimulus patterns' bring about the development within the organism of a 'neuronal model' of the environment. (40) The removal of familiar patterns results in a tendency to search for them. Their reappearance evokes approach responses. The appearance of new patterns – a mismatch between the model and sensory input – evokes withdrawal from stimulation. This affirms in a modified form the incongruity hypothesis of fear. Thus, the neuronal-model view suggests that at least some withdrawal responses are an after-effect of the establishment of a model of the environment formed during the imprinting process.

Learning generally may be regarded as involving (*a*) some 'sensory impact', and (*b*) an acquisition of some motor response. The former may be inferred from such findings as those concerning 'sensory pre-conditioning' and 'latent learning'; it is also suggested by the introspections of human subjects. What precise effect the sensory impact will have depends on the learner and the learning situation; it could be, for instance, imitation; it could also be imprinting. As for the acquisition of motor patterns, in imprinting, as in classical conditioning, the initial response to stimulation remains essentially unchanged throughout the learning process. In classical conditioning, the original response attaches in the course of learning to new stimuli. In short-term imprinting, the original approach responses simply become restricted to the stimulus type initially encountered.

NOTES

1 K. Lorenz, 'Der Kumpan in der Umwelt des Vogels; Der Artgenosse als auslösendes Moment sozialer Verhaltungsweisen'. *J. Ornithol.*, 1935, *83*, pp. 137–213, 289–413.

2 K. Lorenz, 'The Companion in the Bird's World', *Auk*, 1937, *54*, pp. 245–273.

3 P. Guiton, 'Socialization and Imprinting in Brown Leghorn Chicks', *Anim. Behav.*, 1959, *7*, pp. 26–34.

4 E. A. Salzen and C. C. Meyer, 'Imprinting: Reversal of a Preference Established during the Critical Period', *Nature*, 1967, *215*, pp. 785–786.

5 W. Sluckin, *Imprinting and Early Learning*, 1964, London: Methuen.

6 P. P. G. Bateson, 'The Characteristics and Context of Imprinting', *Biol. Rev.*, 1966, *41*, pp. 177–220.

7 T. B. Collins, 'Strength of the Following Responses in the Chick in Relation to Degree of "Parent" Contact', *J. Comp. Physiol. Psychol.*, 1965, *60*, pp. 192–195.

8 P. H. Klopfer and J. P. Hailman, 'Basic Parameters of Following and Imprinting in Precocial Birds', *Z. Tierpsychol.*, 1964, *21*, pp. 755–762.

9 F. V. Smith and M. W. Bird, 'The Relative Attraction for the Domestic Chick of Combinations of Stimuli in Different Sensory Modalities', *Anim. Behav.*, 1963, *11*, pp. 300–305.

10 W. Sluckin, 'Perceptual and Associative Learning', *Symp. Zool. Soc., Lond.*, 1962, *No. 8*, pp. 193–198.

11 R. J. Andrew, 'The Relation between the Following Response and Precocious Adult Behaviour in the Chick', *Anim. Behav.*, 1966, *14*, pp. 501–505.

12 W. Sluckin and E. A. Salzen, 'Imprinting and Perceptual Learning', *Quart. J. Experim. Psychol.*, 1961, *13*, pp. 65–77.

13 H. S. Hoffman, J. L. Searle, S. Toffey and F. Kozma, 'Behavioral Control by an Imprinted Stimulus', *J. Experim. Anal. Behav.*, 1966, *9*, pp. 177–189.

14 P. H. Klopfer and J. P. Hailman, 'Perceptual Preferences and Imprinting in Chicks', *Science*, 1964, *145*, pp. 1333–1334.

15 P. H. Klopfer, 'Stimulus Preferences and Imprinting', *Science*, 1967, *156*, pp. 1394–1396.

16 Ann Taylor, W. Sluckin and Rosemary Hewitt, 'Changing Colour Preferences of Chicks', *Anim. Behav.*, 1969, *17*, pp. 3–8.

17 Ann Taylor, W. Sluckin, Rosemary Hewitt and P. Guiton, 'The Formation of Attachments by Domestic Chicks to Two Textures', *Anim. Behav.*, 1967, *15*, pp. 514–519.

18 D. O. Hebb, 'On the Nature of Fear', *Psychol. Rev.*, 1946, *53*, pp. 250–275.

19 G. W. Bronson, 'The Fear of Novelty', *Psychol. Bull.*, 1968, *69*, pp. 350–358.

20 P. P. G. Bateson, 'Effect of Similarity between Rearing and Testing Conditions on Chicks Following and Avoidance Responses', *J. Comp. Physiol. Psychol.*, 1964, *57*, pp. 100–103.

21 P. Guiton and W. Sluckin, 'The Effects of Visual Experience on Behavioural Development in Neonatal Chicks', *Br. J. Psychol.*, 1969, *60*, pp. 495–507.

22 S. J. Dimond, 'Personal Communication'.

23 F. Schutz, 'Die Bedeutung früher sozialer Eindrücke während der "Kinder- und Jugendzeit" bie Enten', *Z. Experim. Angew. Psychol.*, 1964, *11*, pp. 169–178.

24 F. Schutz, 'Sexuelle Prägung bei Anatiden', *Z. Tierpsychol.*, 1965, *22*, pp. 50–103.

25 M. W. Schein, 'On the Irreversibility of Imprinting', *Z. Tierpsychol.*, 1963, *20*, pp. 462–467.

26 R. J. Andrew, 'The Development of Adult Responses from Responses Given during Imprinting by the Domestic Chick, *Anim. Behav.*, 1964, *12*, pp. 542–548.

27 R. J. Andrew, 'Precocious Adult Behaviour in the Young Chick', *Anim. Behav.*, 1966, *14*, pp. 485–500.

28 J. de Lannoy, 'Zur Prägung von Instinkthandlungen (Untersuchungen an Stockenten *Anas Platyrhynchos L.* und Kolbenenten *Netta Rufina* Pallas', *Z. Tierpsychol.*, 1967, *24*, pp. 162–300.

29 F. Schutz, 'Homosexualität und Prägung', *Psychol. Forsch.*, 1965, *28*, pp. 439–463.

30 C. O. Whitman, 'The Behavior of Pigeons', in Carr, H. A., ed., *Orthogenetic Evolution of Pigeons*, Vol. 3, 1919, Washington: Carnegie Institute.

31 E. Klinghammer and E. H. Hess, 'Imprinting in an Altricial Bird: the Blond Ring Dove', *Science*, 1964, *146*, pp. 265–266.

32 E. Klinghammer, 'Factors Influencing Choice of Mate in Altricial Birds', in H. W. Stevenson, E. H. Hess and H. L. Rheingold, eds., *Early Behavior: Comparative and Developmental Approaches*, 1967, New York: Wiley.

33 G. Gottlieb, 'Species Identification by Avian Neonates: Con-

tributory Effect of Perinatal Auditory Stimulation', *Anim. Behav.*, 1966, *14*, pp. 282–290.

34 G. J. Fischer, 'Auditory Stimuli in Imprinting', *J. Comp. Physiol. Psychol.*, 1966, *61*, pp. 271–273.

35 J. B. Grier, S. A. Counter and W. M. Shearer, 'Prenatal Auditory Imprinting in Chickens', *Science*, 1967, *155*, pp. 1692–1693.

36 S. J. Dimond, 'Effects of Photic Stimulation Before Hatching on the Development of Fear in Chick', *J. Comp. Physiol. Psychol.*, 1968, *65*, pp. 320–324.

37 E. H. Hess, 'Imprinting in Birds', *Science*, 1964, *146*, pp. 1128–1139.

38 R. A. Hinde, 'Some Aspects of the Imprinting Problem', *Symp. Zool. Soc., Lond., No. 8*, 1962, pp. 129–138.

39 G. J. Fischer, G. L. Campbell and W. M. Davis, 'The Effect of ECS on Retention of Imprinting', *J. Comp. Physiol. Psychol.*, 1965, *59*, pp. 455–457.

40 E. A. Salzen, 'Imprinting and Fear', *Symp. Zool. Soc., London, No. 8*, 1962, pp. 199–217.

CHAPTER 4

Imprinting and Human Behaviour

Classical imprinting studies are concerned with birds. Does imprinting in any sense occur in human beings and other mammals? As already mentioned, a distinction – important for our purpose – can be made between precocial animals, which have functioning sense organs and are capable of locomotion very soon after birth, and altricial animals which are markedly more physically immature at birth. From the standpoint of behavioural development, precocial birds and precocial mammals have much in common. We shall therefore deal with mammals of this type first. Next we shall look at altricial mammals. Finally we shall consider human beings, who fall, of course, into the altricial category. We shall deal with this last task at some length, and we shall treat human imprinting, if there is such, from a number of angles.

I. *Imprinting in precocial mammals*

There is no doubt that approach and following responses are a common occurrence in young precocial mammals. The evidence for actual imprinting is, however, scanty. Over many years, casual observations have been reported of newborn hooved animals following moving figures other than their mothers, for instance, people or cars. More recently, systematic field observations have been conducted; and 'heeling' or following responses in very young moose and elk calves have been described, (1, 2) as well as cases of 'following response to man' in newborn caribou. (3)

Guinea-pigs are more amenable to laboratory observation. In one study infant animals, placed in isolation within hours of birth, were later individually confronted with a white wood-block moving slightly to and fro, and were found to approach this object readily. Other guinea-pigs, that had spent the first few days with their mothers, were put in solitary confinement for two to four days, and then presented with a moving object; these animals, too, showed approach responses. (4) Although these experiments clearly demonstrated approach behaviour in young guinea-pigs, they provided no evidence of imprinting by any of the acceptable criteria.

More recently an experiment was reported in which infant guinea-pigs 5 to 7 days of age were taken away from their mothers, reared in isolation, and also 'trained' daily, some with a tennis ball and some with a black-and-white striped cube of similar size. The training consisted of spending one hour daily with one of these objects, without food or water, for four days in succession; during that time the object moved slowly round in a small circle. On the fifth day each animal was tested for 'preference' between the two objects. It was found that almost all animals made a choice; and when an animal did so, it invariably chose the familiar object. (5) At the time of writing more work with guinea-pigs is in progress; the animals' preferences are studied as a function of the duration of 'exposure-training' and the time-interval between training and testing. (6)

Lambs, too, have been found to develop social attachments to 'perceptually prominent objects' with which these animals had previously been confined; the objects of attachment could be other lambs, dogs, or a television screen displaying various patterns. These particular findings were interpreted in terms of 'associative conditioning', (7) although they might have been considered with as much justification as effects resembling classical imprinting.

It is not altogether clear to what extent imprinting is possible after the first few hours or days after birth. In the case of guinea-pigs prior attachment to the natural mother does not preclude subsequent imprinting to various figures, in the absence of the mother. How strong and lasting such later attachments can be is uncertain. It is also not known up to what age, if there is a limit, such attachments may be formed. These are all matters to be investigated experimentally.

In considering imprinting in precocial mammals, we may mention imprinting-like learning in the adults of some species. Though not early learning, it is a remarkable fact that the females in sheep and goats develop rapidly specific attachments to newborn young, either their own or others. Such attachments appear to result from the exposure of the dam to the specific smell of the lamb or kid in question; and hence – the term 'olfactory imprinting' which has been used to describe the development of such individual mother-to-young ties. It appears that an attachment to strange young animals, i.e. their adoption, occurs only after some days of enforced proximity. (8) The mother-goat has been found to reject its own kid if separated from it after birth for not much longer than an hour; but five minutes of mother-offspring contact after parturition is enough to prevent a rejection of the offspring later, even when a period of some hours of separation has been interposed between the initial contact and the later test of attachment. (9)

II. Social attachments in altricial mammals

As mentioned earlier, so far as imprinting of newborn young to their parents and other figures is concerned, it is studied in precocial rather than altricial mammals because in the former (a) learning through exposure can be more readily separated from conventional reward learning, and (b) the young are soon after birth sufficiently developed to be physically capable of responding in recognition and/or discrimination tests. To be able to recognize anything and to show any preferences, the young of altricial mammals must be old enough to have their eyes open and be able to move, by which time they will probably have already learned a fair amount about their environment. Nevertheless exposure training without the customary reinforcing agents can be given to the young of altricial species much as it can be given to guinea-pigs. Indeed, in one form or another, this type of training has been used with mammals, ranging from marsupials to monkeys. Thus, it has been found that in order to tame opossums it is sufficient to raise them in contact with people. The manner of feeding does not appear to matter much in this process. However, the choice of period when contact with people will lead to tameness is of importance; and the crucial period is reported to be between the time when the eyes open and the time of weaning. (10) Attachments to other species thus brought about have been investigated in mice by a number of workers; though in some studies the acquisition of a given preference by mice (for example, for rats) may well have tied up with reward conditioning. (11)

The learning mechanism is not entirely clear in the development of sexual preferences in mice. The experimental findings are that young female mice reared after weaning with both parents take best later in life to mating with males of their own sub-species; but, those reared only by their mothers mate equally readily with males of their own or of another sub-species. (12) In another study, features of homosexual behaviour were found in female mice reared by their mothers only, but hardly any such tendency was observed in control animals reared normally. (13) The relative sexual attractiveness to females of familiar types of male or female has been ascribed by Mainardi, who has made a study of such phenomena, to sexual imprinting.

Extensive studies have been conducted into the socialization and taming of cats and dogs, particularly the latter. The so-called primary socialization is said to occur in puppies between the ages of about three weeks and some seven to ten weeks. At that time puppies can become attached to dogs, or to people (i.e. can become tame), or to both. (14) Exposure to another species (e.g. human beings) appears to be the necessary and sufficient condition for the formation of attachment by the puppy to that species. In more recent years students of this area of animal behaviour have tended to regard such early learning as essentially imprinting-like in character (or look upon imprinting as equivalent to primary socialization). (15)

It has been known for some time that in infant monkeys 'contact-comfort' rather than food provides the basis for the development of attachment to 'mother' figures. (16) It may be wondered whether such attachments are in part based on an imprinting process, whereby tactile and visual exposure to a 'cloth mother' combine to 'tie' the infant to her. Now in the early days, when imprinting was still regarded as typically a process characterized by rapidity and irreversibility, students of social development in monkeys and apes did not think of infantile attachments as having any affinity to imprinting. More recently, however, research workers studying behaviour development in infra-human primates have been suggesting themselves that imprinting might be an important ingredient of early learning in monkeys. (17)

III. *Imprinting in human infants?*

An early reference to imprinting in human infants was a suggestion that in babies the smiling response, instead of the following response, could be at the root of imprinted attachments. Just as in nidifugous birds approach and following behaviour serves as a basis for the formation of social bonds, so the 'directed' smiling of infants – it was argued – provided the initial ties with the mother and other individuals. (18) In this light, deprivation of maternal affection in infancy could be seen as tantamount to the absence of specific imprinting. These were interesting but wholly tentative and speculative thoughts.

Later, a much more precise assertion was made about human imprinting. An experiment was reported in which the normal heart-beat sound (i.e. 72 paired beats per minute) had been presented at high intensity, day and night, for four days running, to ordinary newborn babies. A control group consisted of babies not exposed to this sound. It was found that the experimental subjects gained more weight, and cried less, than the control ones. In a further experiment some older infants, ranging in age from one to four years, were exposed to 72 paired beats per minute, while groups of control subjects were exposed respectively to no sound at all, to the sound of a metronome, to 72 single beats per minute, and to lullabies. The experimental subjects fell asleep more quickly than those in various control groups. (19) It was considered that infants preferred the heart-beat sound to any other; and it was concluded that auditory imprinting to heart-beat occurs in the foetus inside the mother's womb. This view concerning human intra-uterine imprinting has since received a good deal of publicity. (20, 21)

Two points must be considered separately: the experimental findings, and the inference drawn from them. The findings are no doubt of considerable interest, but they have not so far been replicated. One carefully controlled investigation failed to reveal any increase in weight in young babies exposed to the heart-beat sound, as compared with control subjects; and exposure to heart-beat did not bring about any decrease in activity or a diminution of crying. (22) However, whatever the beneficial effects of exposure to the mother's heart beat or a simulation of it may be, there is no reason why they should result from imprinting *in utero*. A preference for this type of sound could, of course, be genetically based. Only if it were possible to have control subjects *not* exposed to the heart-beat sound in the womb, could any difference between them and normal infants be possibly ascribed to auditory imprinting. Since this is not practicable, we must suspend judgement as to whether imprinting *in utero* takes place.

Suggestive evidence for imprinting of this kind is also sometimes cited. Thus, mothers have been observed to hold their babies on the left side, close to the heart, much more than on the right side; and this has been seen not only in right-handed women, but also left-handed ones. (19) The great majority of people are of course right-handed, and the actual number of left-handed mothers in the study in question appears to have been only 32. It is possible that a survey of a larger number of left-handed mothers would reveal that the tendency among them to hold babies on the left is less marked or absent. For one may expect that both right- and left-handed people are apt to leave the dextrous hand, whichever it is, free for manipulative action. In any case, however, the reasons for carrying infants on the left may have nothing to do with the infants' imprinted preference for heart beat; and the left-handers' conformity with the right-handers could have social-cultural origins. And again, the report that in the madonna-and-child paintings the child is found to be held on the left in 80 per cent of the cases (19) in itself clearly provides no real support for the contention that infants are imprinted to the sound of heart beat. Thus, the question of auditory imprinting of this nature in human beings remains an open one.

IV.   *Imprinting-like human early learning*

In spite of all that has been said, the suggestion that imprinting may play a part in early human learning is not unreasonable. Traditionally, students of child development have tended to stress the role of satisfiers and annoyers even in the earliest learning. Both the psychoanalytic and the learning-theory approaches are alike, in their different ways, in this respect. The feeding experience has been said to be the basis of sociability. (23) Views concerning the nature of the child's tie to its mother – deriving from psychoanalysis – tend to regard dependency on physiological gratification as the basis of the child's growing attachment to the mother-figure. (24) Those who believe that procedures of operant conditioning suggest a valid analysis of the child's early learning see the probable reinforcers of behaviour primarily in food and water, and additionally also in tactile stimuli, taste, skin temperature, and so on, as well as in changes in stimulation in general. (25)

However, a continued extension of the range of possible reinforcers represents a departure from the earlier established conception of motivation of behaviour. Notions such as 'competence motivation' (26) and 'motivation inherent in information processing and action' (27) have been introduced to account for observational and experimental findings which do not readily fit in with the older motivational-theory formulations. The new approaches do not require learning to be tied to such concepts as drive reduction, or even reinforcement. Some learning, at any rate, may be a direct result of exposure to stimulation. Imprinting and, as we shall see in a later chapter, some forms of imitation, may be in this category.

The human infant appears to cry at about three months of age for 'almost any form of environmental change'; it cries at five months 'for the attention of any person'; it cries at ten months specifically 'for his mother'. (28) The particular attachment develops gradually from a general proximity-seeking tendency, and it depends in this development on exposure to the mother-figure. Such a development of affectional ties appears to be akin to imprinting. Early social learning of this type in the human infant has been compared to the socialization of the puppy. It has been said that, like the puppy, the human infant 'at the proper period of life will become attached to anything in the surrounding environment, both living and non-living'. (29)

The equating of attachment to the mother-figure with dependency has also been questioned by implication by students of child development not in the least concerned with imprinting. These workers ascribe attachment in part to dependence on physiological gratification, but in part also to 'the infant's perceptual transactions with its environment'. This view emphasizes 'the role of distance receptors' in the growth of social responsiveness. (30) Since attachment behaviour which develops in the early years may well influence later the individual's sexual and parental behaviour, the study of the development of attachments would appear to be central to the study of personality. (31)

It may be helpful at this point to note that the concept of dependency implies (*a*) dependent behaviour, which might be described as satellization, (32) and (*b*) the causes of such behaviour, that is, its dependence on gratification or reinforcement. The concept of attachment is free from the second of the two implications of dependency. Furthermore, attachment suggests behaviour broader in scope than satellite-like behaviour; for it could refer to ties other than subordinate ones; it could refer to attachments to inanimate things, as well as living, as in imprinting to the physical environment of the subject.

Attachment shows itself in the first place in the seeking of proximity to a specific salient figure which, more often than not, is the mother. Such attachment often remains strong even in the face of ill-treatment by parents; and separation may lead to deep anxiety. Attempts are being made to analyse the development of human social attachments in terms of imprinting and other facets of early learning in animals. (33) It may also be fruitful to consider more closely the lasting effects of human early social learning with reference to the relevant findings of animal-behaviour studies. However, whether the growth of attachments in human beings has much or little to do with classical imprinting, it is certainly a learning process that requires much further study. And rather than be preoccupied with 'labelling' the formative learning processes early in life, it is important to continue to study systematically the diversity of factors involved in the development of social bonds among individuals.

NOTES

1   M. Altmann, 'Social Integration in the Moose Calf', *Anim. Behav.*, 1958, *6*, pp. 155–159.

2   M. Altmann, 'Naturalistic Studies of Maternal Care in Moose and Elk', in *Maternal Behavior in Mammals*, 1963, ed. H. L. Rheingold, New York: Wiley.

3   P. C. Lent, 'Calving and Related Social Behavior in the Barren-ground Caribou', Z. *Tierpsychol.*, 1966, *23*, pp. 701–756.

4   W. U. Shipley, 'The Demonstration in the Domestic Guinea-pig of a Process Resembling Classical Imprinting', *Anim. Behav.*, 1963, *11*, pp. 470–474.

5   W. Sluckin, 'Imprinting in Guinea-pigs', *Nature*, 1968, *220*, p. 1148.

6   W. Sluckin and Clare Fullerton, 'Attachments of infant guinea-pigs', *Psychon. Sci.*, 1969, *17*, pp. 179–180.

7   R. B. Cairns, 'Development, Maintenance, and Extinction of Social Attachment Behavior in Sheep', *J. Comp. Physiol. Psychol.*, 1966, *62*, pp. 298–306.

8.   L. Hersher, J. B. Richmond and A. U. Moore, 'Modifiability of the Critical Period for the Development of Maternal Behaviour in Sheep and Goats', *Behaviour*, 1963, *20*, pp. 311–320.

9   P. H. Klopfer, D. K. Adams and M. S. Klopfer, 'Maternal "Imprinting" in Goats', *Proc. Natn. Acad. Sci., U.S.A.*, 1964, *52*, pp. 911–914.

10   H. Friedman, 'Taming of Virginia Opossum', *Nature*, 1964, *201*, pp. 323–324.

11   V. H. Denenberg, G. A. Hudgens and M. X. Zarrow, 'Mice Reared With Rats: Modification of Behavior by Early Experience with Another Species', *Science*, 1964, *143*, pp. 380–381.

12   D. Mainardi, 'Eliminazione della barriera etologica all'isolamento riproduttivo tra *Mus musculus domesticus* et *Mus musculus bactrianus* mediante ezione sull'apprendimento infantile', *Instituto Lombardo (Rend. Sci.)*, 1963, *97*, pp. 291–299.

13   D. Mainardi, 'Rapporti tra apprendimenti infantile e omosexualitá nella femmina di topo', *Arch. Zool. Ital.*, 1963, *48*, pp. 137–145.

14   J. P. Scott, *Animal Behaviour*, 1958, Chicago: University of Chicago Press.

15   J. P. Scott and J. L. Fuller, *Genetics and the Social Behavior of the Dog*, 1965, Chicago: University of Chicago Press.

16   H. F. Harlow and R. R. Zimmerman, 'Affectional Responses in the Infant Monkey', *Science*, 1959, *130*, pp. 421–432.

17   G. P. Sackett, M. Porter and H. Holmes, 'Choice Behavior, in Rhesus Monkeys: Effect of Stimulation During the First Month of Life', *Science*, 1965, *147*, pp. 304–306.

18   P. H. Gray, 'Theory and Evidence of Imprinting in Human Infants', *J. Psychol.*, 1958, *46*, pp. 155–166.

19   L. Salk, 'Mother's Heartbeat as an Imprinting Stimulus', *Trans. N. Y. Acad. Sci.*, 1962, *24*, pp. 753–763.

20   L. Salk, 'Thoughts on the Concept of Imprinting and its Place in

Early Human Development, *Canad. Psychiat. Assoc. J.*, 1966, *11*, pp. 295–305.

21 D. Morris, *The Naked Ape*, 1967, London: Cape.

22 J. D. Tulloch, B. C. Brown, H. L. Jacobs, D. G. Prugh and W. A. Greene, 'Normal Heartbeat Sound and the Behavior of Newborn Infants – a Replication Study', *Psychosom. Med.*, 1964, *26*, pp. 661–670.

23 J. Dollard and N. E. Miller, *Personality and Psychotherapy*, 1950, New York: McGraw-Hill.

24 J. Bowlby, 'The Nature of the Child's Tie to his Mother', *Internat. J. Psychoanal.*, 1958, *39*, pp. 1–24.

25 S. W. Bijou and D. M. Baer, *Child Development, Vol. II*, 1965, New York: Appleton-Century-Crofts.

26 R. W. White, 'Motivation Reconsidered: the Concept of Competence', *Psychol. Rev.*, 1959, *66*, pp. 297–330.

27 J. McV. Hunt, 'Motivation Inherent in Information Processing and Action', in *Motivation and Social Interaction*, ed. D. J. Harvey, 1963, New York: Ronald Press.

28 H. R. Schaffer, 'Some Issues for Research in the Study of Attachment Behaviour', in *Determinants of Infant Behaviour, II*, ed. B. M. Foss, 1963, London: Methuen.

29 J. P. Scott, 'The Process of Primary Socialization in Canine and Human Infants', *Monogr. Soc. Res. Child Devel.*, 1963, *28*, No. 1, pp. 1–47.

30 R. H. Walters and R. D. Parke, 'The Role of Distance Receptors in the Development of Social Responsiveness', in *Advances in Child Development and Behavior*, Vol. 2, eds. L. P. Lipsitt and C. C. Spiker, 1965, New York: Academic Press.

31 J. Bowlby, 'The Child's Tie to his Mother: a Review of Recent Work and Theory', *Bull. Br. Psychol. Soc.*, 1967, *20*, (66), pp. 42–43.

32 D. P. Ausubel, *Ego Development and the Personality Disorders*, 1952, New York: Grune and Stratton.

33 E. A. Salzen, 'Imprinting in Birds and Primates', *Behaviour*, 1967, *28*, pp. 232–254.

CHAPTER 5

Reactivity and Docility

So far we have been dealing with early learning of specific responses (as in conditioning) or preferences (as in imprinting). We shall now turn to the early acquisition of more general features of behaviour: activity and reactivity. We shall also consider in a selective manner the influence of early experience upon subsequent behavioural development.

I. *Habituation and reactivity*

An animal subjected to new stimulation shows some form of orienting response: selective attention, startle, aversive behaviour. Orientation responses weaken as the particular stimulus is repeatedly presented. This is an elementary learning process – extinction of the orientation reflex, or habituation. It tends to be specific to any given stimuli in any modality. Habituation is a short-term process. In the long run there is a spontaneous recovery of responsiveness. More immediately, there tends to be some generalized habituation to stimulation, that is a reduction in responsiveness to stimuli other than those actually experienced. Could there also be longer-term generalized habituation resulting from the impact of early experiences? Research findings suggest that this may be the case.

One type of stimulation much used in the laboratory with the young of small mammals, such as mice and rats, consists in handling the animals, or in the so-called gentling (that is, handling and stroking). The effects of such experiences may be regarded as delayed generalized habituation, or decreased emotionally in later life. The term, emotionality, in relation to animals, has a some-what anthropomorphic ring; it actually refers to behaviour exhibiting marked reactivity, including signs of fear, in response to many forms of stimulation. Such behaviour can be defined operationally, e.g. in terms of ambulation and defaecation in an open-field test, and appropriate definitions of emotionality and reactivity have, in fact, been given by those who are advancing the study of long-term effects of various infantile experiences of animals. (1, 2, 3, 4)

At the risk of over-simplification, it may be said that both ex-posure to specific stimuli, e.g. bell-ringing, and exposure to rela-tively non-specific stimulation, e.g. handling, produce – at least in rodents – essentially the same later-life behavioural effects; broadly, what happens is that extra-stimulation in infancy reduces the animals' later reactivity. Noxious stimulation, such as electric shocks, acts in a similar manner. (5) These findings suggest that it is stimulation as such, rather than stimulation of some particular variety, that brings about later in life the relative quiesence in the face of environmental change.

Whenever infantile stimulation influences the later emotional or motivational state of the animal, we are dealing with early-experience effects. However, in so far as these effects may be re-garded as continuous with, or an extension of, habituation (that is – as generalized long-term habituation), they may be described as early-learning phenonmena. Something could be said in favour of either conceptualization.

II. *Early experience and later exploratory behaviour*

Low reactivity to novelty in animals, or human beings, does not entail a lack of interest in novelty. Somewhat paradoxically, quite the contrary may be the case. Subjects that startle less readily, that 'freeze up' less, that do not show fear of new stimuli, are the very ones that are the most apt to investigate and explore. This has been established in rodents; in these species reactivity may be increased, while the exploratory tendency is decreased, by restric-tion of stimulation in infancy, that is, by solitary rearing conditions and a generally monotonous early environment. The responsive individuals are not neccessarily the interested ones.

Studies conducted as far back as the early fifties showed that mature mice isolated in infancy, were less investigatory than those initially reared by the mother, that is, than animals with seemingly richer early experience. (6) More recently, it was reported that previously unhandled rats were less visually exploratory than the more stimulated, handled ones. (7) There are quite a few reports in the literature pointing in this direction, though findings are sometimes equivocal. However, studies of dogs seem to contradict any such general conclusions. Puppies raised singly in isolation were found at 7 to 10 months to be more active and more curious than normally reared young dogs. Even several years later dogs initially maternally deprived differed to some degree in this way from normal animals. (8, 9) It has been suggested that this type of over-curiosity resulting from solitary rearing indicates a lack of intelligence. This could be concluded from the slowness at reward-learning and at avoidance-learning evident in some animals that had prolonged periods of isolation in infancy. However, systematic research has shown that deprivation does not necessarily prevent the development of intelligent behaviour in every dog. And in any case it has been established that short breaks in isolation, even at infrequent intervals, can effectively counteract the ill-effects of this mode of rearing. (10)

III. *Perceptual development*

Many writers have expressed the view that perceiving is not just a matter of the presence of sensory capacities coupled with effective sensory stimulation. Indeed, it has been said that the full ability to perceive develops only with perceptual experience, or that powers of perception depend on perceptual learning. In this sense, the phrase 'perceptual learning' refers to the gradual process of learning to perceive (and not, as in other contexts, to the role of perception in learning). Does, in fact, perceptual learning benefit much from early exposure to stimulation? There are many indications that it does; although it must be borne in mind that perceptual development is inferred from the observed development of behaviour, and that in making such inferences there is much room for doubt and uncertainty.

The effectiveness of early sensory experience has been studied in a number of species. It was found that rats which in infancy had had visual experience of specific patterns (such as triangles, crosses, etc.) were later better at two-dimensional form discriminations than inexperienced animals. (11) Likewise with auditory patterns: rats raised in soundproof lockers were found to be less good than normally reared animals at solving some auditory pattern discrimination problems. (12) Rather more controversial is the influence of early experience on the perception of pain. Puppies reared in isolation until maturity were found to be slower at making proper avoidance responses than normally reared animals. Furthermore, slow responses of the 'deprived dogs' in nose-burning and pin-pricking tests suggested that not only the learning ability but also the capacity to perceive pain might be impaired in animals whose early sensory experiences had been restricted. (13)

It may be concluded from studies such as these, as well as from investigations of imprinting in precocial birds, that exposure to stimulation of one kind or another very early in life could have a marked effect on perceptual development, for example, the development of powers of discrimination. (14) It may be said that early sensory deprivation has both perceptual and learning repercussions later in life in that it '. . . prevents the formation of adequate models and strategies for dealing with the environment. . . .' (15)

IV. *Learning to learn*

It appears that laboratory animals isolated in infancy, or otherwise environmentally restricted, tend to be handicapped in their perceptual development relative to those with more varied stimulation in infancy (such as may result from handling, social contact, and so on). Likewise, with regard to later learning abilities, animal subjects restricted in experience early on are handicapped later in life. Many studies have been carried out in this field since the middle nineteen-fifties on mice and rats. The findings bear out the difficulty of generalizing too readily. Experience of a complex free environment improves such later problem-solving abilities as are needed in, for instance, the running of mazes. Handled or shocked infant rodents, and kittens, are in some cases better, but in other cases less good than relatively unstimulated animals at avoidance learning. (16, 17) This need not be altogether surprising since such learning may be more difficult for experienced and well-habituated subjects than for the 'naïve' ones who more promptly respond to novelty by withdrawal and avoidance.

Whereas earlier studies tended to be concerned with fairly general effects of early experience upon the later learning powers of animals, the more recent ones have paid more attention to the influence of various forms of early stimulation upon different types of learning task. One investigation of mice, for instance, has shown that different amounts of pre-weaning stimulation could have varying effects on different learning tasks in accordance with their difficulty; a good deal of early stimulation would appear to result later in comparatively slow learning of easy tasks, but could be instrumental in bringing about quite fast learning of difficult tasks. (18) Findings of this kind, as well as those showing differential effects of enriched environment on 'bright' and 'dull' animal and human subjects, suggest the need for a further analysis of the circumstances in which positive transfer of experience and learning is operative. (19, 20)

It looks as if varied early environment provides opportunities for early learning, which is then transferred to later adult learning. Variety of early experience appears to provide the conditions for the making and breaking of learning sets, that is, broadly, for flexible adaptive modes of later behaviour. (21) Furthermore, the effects of such early experience are seemingly not easily offset by whatever happens later. What is learned, and the sequence of learning early in life, can be influential. While essentially reversible, early learning may be in some ways disproportionately effective; that is, early learning may sometimes be important because of its primacy. (22) It is a matter for further research, slow and painstaking though it may be, to establish when precisely the primacy effect is a reality and how it operates.

V. Early deprivation and early learning

The study of some of the effects of early deprivation in animals can shed light on the role of early learning in the development of behaviour. Some kinds of deprivation and some of its effects are only marginally relevant to the theme of this book. The so-called drive deprivation is in this category: this includes hunger in infancy, early weaning, sucking frustration, etc. Deprivation of what has been called dependency drive is another matter. The traditional learning-theory view suggests that this could be an acquired drive for proximity to mother-figure which results from continued reinforcement of contact with that figure. As mentioned in the last chapter, another approach, which derives from imprinting and socialization studies, is to regard dependency behaviour as an expression of attachment to a figure caused by 'self-reinforcing' exposure to it. In any case, the absence of attachment-attracting figures early in life is tantamount to deprivation of early learning, and this influences greatly the subject's later social behaviour. This is borne out by experimental findings such as are quoted below.

Deprivation of attachment (or frustration of dependency drive) tends to have certain typical repercussions in many species. In the Burmese Red Jungle-fowl, for instance, social deprivation results in the channelling of aggression towards the self (own tail) and to other species, and leads to abnormal stereotyping of behaviour, including sexual fixations. (23) In dogs early restriction and social isolation result in later abnormalities of responses to visual, auditory, olfactory and noxious stimuli, as well as in later difficulty in inhibiting 'irrelevant' responses, and in some asocial behaviour, including the absence of any genuine tameness. (24, 25) In the rhesus monkey, such early deprivation affects adversely – and in a striking manner – the animals' exploratory behaviour; it also, if less so, adversely affects the animals' social behaviour and to some limited extent their learning abilities. (26) The damage to social behaviour is severe if the early social deprivation is complete and prolonged. But the absence of a mother-figure may be compensated by the presence of peers, while the ill-effects of the lack of peers may be made up by good relationship with the mother. (27)

We have already seen that stimulus deprivation is detrimental to perceptual development. This must be interpreted in a broad manner. Thus visual stimulation as well as experience of movement in space contribute to the development of visual functioning. (28) Lack of diversity in early environment results in excessive fear of novelty later in life; and maternal deprivation may be an important factor in impoverishing early experience. The consequent fearfulness, whether in animals or in man, is likely in turn to have a restrictive influence on cognitive experience and cognitive development. (29) Thus, a good deal of early learning to perceive, to act and to inhibit action would seem to be necessary for the full development of the individual's potentialities. What may be said to be known, and what has been hypothesized, about the role of early learning in young children, or how early learning appears to influence personality development, will be considered in Chapter 9.

NOTES

1 C. S. Hall and P. H. Whitman, 'The Effects of Infantile Stimulation upon Later Emotional Stability in the Mouse', *J. Comp. Physiol. Psychol.*, 1951, *44*, pp. 61–66.

2 S. Levine, 'Emotionality and Aggressive Behavior in the Mouse as a Function of Infantile Experience', *J. Genet. Psychol.*, 1959, *94*, pp. 77–83.

3 V. H. Denenberg, 'Early Experience and Emotional Development', *Sci. Amer.*, 1963, *208*, pp. 138–146.

4 J. J. Cowley and E. M. Widdowson, 'The Effect of Handling Rats on their Growth and Behaviour', *Br. J. Nutr.*, 1965, *19*, pp. 394–406.

5 V. H. Denenberg, 'The Interactive Effects of Infantile and Adult Shock Levels upon Learning', *Psychol. Rep.*, 1959, *5*, pp. 357–364.

6 M. W. Kahn, 'Infantile Experience and Mature Aggressive Behavior of Mice: Some Maternal Influences', *J. Genet. Psychol.*, 1954, *84*, pp. 65–75.

7 G. Y. DeNelsky and V. H. Denenberg, 'Infantile Stimulation and Adult Exploratory Behavior in the Rat: Effects of Handling upon Visual Variation-seeking', *Anim. Behav.*, 1967, *15*, pp. 568–573.

8 W. R. Thompson and W. Heron, 'The Effect of Early Restriction on Activity in Dogs', *J. Comp. Physiol. Psychol.*, 1954, *47*, pp. 77–82.

9 W. R. Thompson and R. Melzack, 'Early Environment', *Sci. Amer.*, 1956, *194*, pp. 38–42.

10 J. L. Fuller, 'Experimental Deprivation and Later Behavior', *Science*, 1967, *158*, pp. 1645–1652.

11 R. H. Forgus, 'Advantage of Early over Late Perceptual Experience in Improving Form Discrimination', *Canad. J. Psychol.*, 1956, *10*, pp. 147–155.

12 R. C. Tees, 'Effects of Early Auditory Restriction in the Rat on Adult Pattern Discrimination', *J. Comp. Physiol. Psychol.*, 1967, *63*, pp. 389–393.

13 R. Melzack and T. H. Scott, 'The Effects of Early Experience on the Response to Pain', *J. Comp. Physiol. Psychol.*, 1957, *50*, pp. 155–161.

14 P. P. G. Bateson, 'An Effect of Imprinting on the Perceptual Development of Domestic Chicks', *Nature*, 1964, *202*, pp. 421–422.

15 J. S. Bruner, 'The Cognitive Consequences of Early Sensory Deprivation', *Psychosom. Med.*, 1959, *21*, pp. 89–95.

16 V. H. Denenberg and R. W. Bell, 'Critical Periods for the Effects of Infantile Experience on Adult Learning, *Science*, 1960, *131*, pp. 227–228.

17 M. Wilson, J. M. Warren and L. Abbott, 'Infantile Stimulation, Activity and Learning by Cats', *Child Devel.*, 1965, *36*, pp. 843–853.

18 A. M. Smith, 'Infantile Stimulation and the Yerkes-Dodson Law', *Canad. J. Psychol.*, 1967, *21*, pp. 285–293.

19 R. M. Cooper and J. P. Lubek, 'Effects of Enriched and Restricted Early Environments on the Learning Ability of Bright and Dull Rats', *Canad. J. Psychol.*, 1958, *12*, pp. 159–164.

20 A. D. B. Clarke and C. B. Blakemore, 'Age and Perceptual-motor Transfer in Imbeciles', *Br. J. Psychol.*, 1961, *52*, pp. 125–131.

21 A. S. Luchins and R. H. Forgus, 'The Effect of Differential Postweaning Environment on the Rigidity of an Animal's Behaviour', *J. Genet. Psychol.*, 1955, *86*, pp. 51–58.

22 A. J. Nyman, 'Problem Solving in Rats as a Function of Experience at Different Ages', *J. Genet. Psychol.*, 1967, *110*, pp. 31–39.

23 J. P. Kruijt, 'Ontogeny of Social Behaviour in Burmese Red Junglefowl', *Behaviour*, 1964, Supplement XII, pp. 1–201.

24 J. P. Scott, 'The Process of Primary Socialization in Canine and Human Infants', *Monogr. Soc. Res. Child Devel.*, 1963, *28* (No. 1), pp. 1–47.

25 R. Melzack, 'Early Experience: a Neuropsychological Approach to Heredity-environment Interactions', in *Early Experience and Behaviour*, eds. G. Newton and S. Levine, 1968, Springfield, Ill.: C. C. Thomas.

26 G. A. Griffin, 'Effects of Three Months of Total Social Deprivation on Social Adjustment and Learning in the Rhesus Monkey', *Child Devel.*, 1966, *37*, pp. 533–547.

27 H. F. Harlow and M. K. Harlow, 'Effects of Mother-infant Relationships on Rhesus Monkey Behaviours', in *Determinants of Infant Behaviour: IV*, ed. B. M. Foss, 1969, London: Methuen.

28 U. Bronfenbrenner, 'Early Deprivation in Mammals: a Cross-species Analysis', in *Early Experience and Behavior*, eds. G. Newton and S. Levine, 1968, Springfield, Ill.: C. C. Thomas.

29 G. W. Bronson, 'The Development of Fear in Man and other Animals', *Child Devel.*, 1968, *39*, pp. 409–431.

CHAPTER 6

Sensitive Periods

A distinction must be drawn between developmental stages in behaviour and sensitive periods. The latter is a narrower term, and refers to those stages in development when the organism is especially susceptible to environmental influences. (1) Only some of the environmental influences bring about learning. The sensitive period for learning of any kind is the time in the development of the animal or person when the particular form of learning can most readily take place.

I. *Development and learning*

The word 'development' refers to directional changes of structure and function associated with growth (and with ageing). Developmental changes of behaviour early in life are rooted in physical development; and the latter consists of growth *per se* as well as of differentiation of function accompanying growth, i.e. maturation. Developmental changes are also influenced by stimulation impinging upon the individual, or experience, including learning. At the time at which learning begins to be effective the individual already displays certain forms of behaviour. These initial ways of responding to stimulation, together with the organism's innate capacities, delimit what the individual can learn. Learning may thus be viewed as a progressive modification and adaptation of early modes of behaviour to the continuing external and internal stimulation.

Stimuli, whether visual, auditory, or any other, make some impact upon the young organism; they evoke an emotional toning and they elicit responses which may be classified into either approach or withdrawal reactions. Approach and withdrawal relative to the source of stimulation, that is proximity-seeking and proximity-avoidance, can be regarded as the two basic types of action. (2) Some students of animal behaviour claim that stimulation of moderate intensity tends to bring about approach while intense stimulation causes withdrawal. However, such a generalization is uninformative in that stimulation relative to the organism would be defined as intense when it evokes withdrawal and as moderate when it evokes approach; that is, intensity of stimulation cannot be defined independently of behaviour.

The two gross patterns of movement, approach and withdrawal, appear to be superimposed upon less pronounced and less clearly directed activity. This background activity may be described as random, although on analysis it might be found to consist of slight abient and adient movements in relation to the plethora of discernible environmental stimuli. The level of this random activity is, in principle, assessable; indeed, attempts at measuring such activity in animals, and even in human infants, have a long history. (3) The level of general activity is related, among other things, to the age of the organism; generally there is a progressive decline in random activity and an increase in specific activity. Activity depends also on the level of sensory input (sometimes equated with arousal or activation); broadly, non-arousing monotonous sensory stimulation tends to depress activity and induce sleep. It may be noted for instance that even quite slight differences in the character of visual stimulation have been found to affect markedly the level of activity in young domestic chicks. (4) Is the responsiveness of the young animal related to its random general activity? On the one hand, there is evidence that the active individual is more alert and more likely to show approach and withdrawal behaviour when appropriately stimulated. On the other hand, a given stimulus is more salient under conditions of lower general stimulation; and since it is more salient, such a stimulus is more likely to bring about a movement towards or away from its source in a relatively inactive organism than in an active one.

Random activity, approach responses and withdrawal responses are the beginnings of behaviour. Early experience moulds it from the start, influencing the individual's reactivity and his ability to learn. But behavioural development is not necessarily smooth and steady. If so, then we may ask about any kind of early experience when precisely it is influential. Above all, it is of great interest to know at what periods in early development learning of one or another kind can occur.

II. *The concept of critical period*

Sensitive periods for learning are not infrequently called critical periods. The latter is the stronger phrase of the two, and it implies that unless learning occurs during the period in question, it will never occur. This may, in fact, be so in some cases, but clearly, not all sensitive periods are critical in the strict sense. Indeed, as we shall see, very often sensitive periods are merely optimal periods for learning, and only sometimes may sensitive periods be described with justification as critical.

Some writers tend to use the term 'critical periods' rather too readily, and somewhat misleadingly, in relation to particular learning situations. They talk of critical periods when special sensitivity rather than criticality has been established. Since critical periods for learning are *ipso facto* sensitive periods, it is probably safer to use the latter term in all but extreme cases. However, variations in terminology need not at all be regarded as posing a serious problem. What really matters are the empirical findings and the conclusions which may be drawn from them.

Before attempting to look at what is known about sensitive periods for early learning it may be useful to consider the scope of our brief survey. In one sense the Freudian view that personality is moulded as the child passes through the sequence of the so-called psycho-sexual stages is concerned with early learning. However, the testing of psychoanalytic hypotheses of this type is difficult and none too conclusive; and such research is not quite in the same category as the less ambitious but more specific forms of obser- vational and experimental research with which we must be primarily concerned. Nor can we attempt a survey of other theses relating to development, such as Piaget's, which have certain implications for early learning.

On the other hand, the experimental studies in the field of

behaviour development which are concerned with the effects of stimulation (such as handling, shocks, etc.) at different ages upon later behaviour have perhaps greater claim for inclusion in our review. As we have seen earlier, it is open to debate how far such effects could be included under the heading of learning; and narrowly interpreted, learning would not encompass these phenomena. However, the criticality of early stimulation is of much interest and relevance to the topic of early learning. At one time the view was quite widely held that, at least in some species, stimulation is most effective in the period immediately following birth. (5) There is now much uncertainty on this point, and we shall return to this problem briefly in the last section of this chapter.

III. Some findings and views

A sensitive period in the development of song patterns in certain bird species occurs in 'adolescence', and song-learning at that time appears to be irreversible. Experimental studies of chaffinches show that young males learn some features of their song from adult males during the first few weeks of life; subsequently, the details of song patterns are learned by the young birds during the first breeding season. (6) The full song, which combines inborn and acquired sound patterns, is fully developed by the end of the thirteenth month of life, and thereafter remains unaltered. The acquisition of the characteristic details of the song is, in the case of the chaffinch, strictly confined to the later learning period which can be described as critical for song acquisition.

The song development in several other bird species has also been studied. Learning plays a part in some species but not in others. In some cases imitations of songs of other species are added to the specific, innately based song pattern. Learning can take place in the first few months of life, but also later on during certain sensitive periods. (1) Although such learning occurs mostly before maturity, it is not a learning that typically takes place in infancy, and so it is doubtful whether it should be classed as early learning.

Not much is as yet known about the role of learning in the development of mammalian vocalizations. Other abilities where an innate capacity provides a foundation for learning have, however, been studied in mammals. Nest-building by apes is an example. Adult chimpanzees, gorillas and orangutans·construct in the wild a sleeping platform or nest every night, while youngsters sleep with mothers. Infant chimpanzees show first attempts at nest building when rather less than a year old. At about two years of age the youngsters practise at it a great deal. They cease sleeping with their mothers when about 3 to 4 years old, by which time the young animals are capable of making adequate nests of their own. (7) It appears that much early learning is needed for the mastery of the skill of nest building. It has been found that in captivity, without the relevant experience, adult chimpanzees 'with all the required manipulatory skills and considerable interest in both materials and nests produced by cagemates, may require extensive training to acquire the requisite pattern of responses'. (8) Thus, it looks as if there is an early sensitive period in chimpanzees for the learning of nest building, even although some later acquisition of this skill is, to a degree, possible.

It used to be thought that an example *par excellence* of the sensitive or critical period was to be found in classical imprinting. Even relatively recently an eminent ethologist stated that 'the strongest and most complete imprinting can only be attained during this critical period, the length of which rarely exceeds some few hours'. (9) However, it has been known for quite some time that, when reared in groups, newly hatched birds, such as domestic chicks, become imprinted to one another and that, after two – or at most three – days, they therefore will no longer be inclined to follow, or tend to become attached to, unfamiliar figures (except after a period of separation from one another). On the other hand, young birds raised in isolation remain susceptible to imprinting for much longer periods than those reared communally. (10) This finding has been repeatedly confirmed, and the conclusion must be drawn that it is misleading to think of imprinting as occurring solely during some short, genetically determined, critical period. (11, 12) The sensitive period for imprinting is thus governed partly by environmental conditions; and under given conditions there are more favourable and less favourable times for the formation of imprinted attachments.

Imprinting refers to attachments to individual figures as well as to the species as a whole. It is not quite clear whether the animal's attachment to its own kind is simply a generalized attachment to individuals. If this is so, then socialization which depends primarily on exposure to other members of the species may be equated with imprinting. Thus the more-or-less sensitive time of socialization in nidifugous birds would be the same as that for imprinting. (13) This is a view that has been quite widely held, but it has to be reconciled with certain experimental findings which indicate that aggregative behaviour in such animals as domestic chicks can be acquired at any time of the individual's development. (14, 15) These findings do not, however, necessarily suggest that socialization is basically different from imprinting; they may perhaps point to imprintability being possible at times other than at the start of life. At the same time, individual imprinting – although not as narrowly confined in time as originally thought – cannot readily be shown to occur in precocial birds after the first several days post-hatch. Thus more research would seem to be called for in this area.

Developmental stages and sensitive periods in the behavioural ontogeny of mammals, such as rodents, have been receiving attention for many years. (16) The dog has probably been studied from the viewpoint of socialization more extensively than any other animal. (17) From some three weeks of age until about ten weeks the puppy is susceptible to socializing influences; at that time 'primary socialization' determines to what living things – including people – the animal will become firmly attached. Other animals, too, have been said to pass through a similar critical period. J. P. Scott contends that the 'critical period for primary socialization constitutes a turning point'. (18) He summarizes the situation as follows: 'Experience during a short period early in life determines which shall be the close relatives of the young animal, and this, in turn, leads the animal to develop in one of two directions – the normal one, in which it becomes attached to and mates with a member of its own species, or an abnormal one, in which it becomes attached to a different species, with consequent disrupting effects upon sexual and other social relationships with members of its own kind'. (18)

This and similar assertions have, however, been challenged. On the basis of a study of young beagles and terriers, the authors of one paper concluded that 'the results do not support the idea of a critical period for especially efficient learning of social responses'. (19) Other workers could find no critical periods for social learning in the cat. (20) And yet the Harlows, referring to the rhesus monkey, said: '. . . our experiments indicate that there is a critical period somewhere between the third and sixth months of life during which social deprivation, particularly deprivation of the company of its peers, irreversibly blights the animal's capacity for social adjustment'. (21) It is possible that the seemingly contradictory statements found in the literature would be more capable of reconciliation if the debate were not so much about critical periods as about sensitive periods, greatly varying in extent from species to species and from one learning situation to another.

Much as in the case of animals, there has been considerable uncertainty about sensitive periods for early learning in children. At the time when attachment to mother was commonly regarded as an instrumentally acquired dependency, the view was expressed that there were two critical periods for socialization: one in the first year of life when the child learns dependency, and the other at 2–3 years of age when the child learns to be independent in certain important respects. Failure to learn at either stage could do irreparable damage. (22) A later suggestion, in tune with some views expressed about imprinting and primary socialization in mammals, was that the process of socialization in human infants begins at some 6 weeks of age but reaches its peak, as indicated by the smiling response, at 4–5 months, and then continues for some time. (23) However, most students of child development, though interested in the possibility of critical periods, remain uncertain and look to more research being done in this field. (24) There may, of course, be sensitive periods for various other forms of learning in children, such as a readiness to learn the native language, a readiness – perhaps – to learn to read, and so on. Clearly, much more systematic research will yet be needed before a body of well attested factual knowledge is gathered together.

IV.   *Some issues for debate*

Sensitive periods for imprinting, or for socialization, or for the acquisition of particular skills have, of course, to do with learning.

The so-called critical periods for stimulation, or – more precisely – for the effectiveness of stimulation, are not necessarily equivalent to sensitive periods for learning. In the case of mice and rats there is some evidence for the existence of effective periods for stimulation; for adult performance of one kind or another may be more influenced by a given type of stimulation at one early stage of development than at another. Assuming that stimulus input in infancy acts to reduce subsequent reactivity, it has been argued that there must be an inverted-U relationship for certain types of task between infantile stimulation and adult performance; (25) that is, as might be expected, there is an optimal level of reactivity for any type of performance. Whether a general predictive theory of infantile stimulation is at present possible is doubtful. What is undoubtedly needed is more factual information which would relate (*a*) the nature and extent of stimulation to which members of a given species are exposed at different developmental stages, and (*b*) the later behaviour of these individuals, that is, their performance on various types of task.

What critical periods for stimulation, if any, there are in human development, is very largely a matter of speculation. It is, of course, entirely to be expected that both the age and the nature of early experience should influence later behaviour. Therefore to talk about sensitive or critical periods for stimulation or learning could be both superfluous and misleading. However this may be, hypotheses concerning specific critical periods could very well be useful in suggesting and directing research. The implications of the critical-period proposition depend on the way it is formulated. While a general statement concerning sensitive periods in human development is not very illuminating, it is at the same time not really contestable. Sharper formulations could lead to empirical studies designed to establish the reality of the hypothesized relations between stimulation, age and later behaviour. However, the research worker probably misconceives his task if he sets out to seek clearly marked critical or even sensitive periods. It is sufficient for any programme of research to set out to specify the relations between the various timings of early stimulation of learning of one kind or another and the different modes of later behaviour. Then, whether such relationships as are discerned deserve to be described in terms of critical periods, or sensitive periods, or any such, becomes mainly a matter of the usage of language.

NOTES

1　R. A. Hinde, *Animal Behaviour: a Synthesis of Ethology and Comparative Psychology*, 1966, New York: McGraw-Hill.
2　T. C. Schneirla, 'An Evolutionary and Developmental Theory of Biphasic Process Underlying Approach and Withdrawal', in *Nebraska Symposium on Motivation*, ed. M. R. Jones, 1959, Lincoln: University of Nebraska Press.
3　O. C. Irwin, 'Amount and Nature of Activities of Newborn Infants under Constant External Stimulating Conditions during the First Ten Days of Life', *Genet. Psychol. Monogr.*, 1930, *8*, pp. 1–92.
4　P. P. G. Bateson, 'Changes in the Activity of Isolated Chicks over the First Week after Hatching', *Anim. Behav.*, 1964, *12*, pp. 490–492.
5　S. Levine, 'Stimulation in Infancy', *Sci. Amer.*, 1960, *202*, pp. 81–86.
6　W. H. Thorpe, 'The Development of Song Patterns by Birds as Evidence for Sensitive Periods in Learning', *Acta Psychol.*, 1964, *23*, p. 100.
7　J. van Lawick-Goodall, 'The Behaviour of Free-living Chimpanzees in the Gombe Stream Reserve', *Animal Behav. Monogr.*, 1968, *1*, pp. 161–311.
8　I. S. Bernstein, 'Age and Experience in Chimpanzee Nest-building', *Psychol. Rep.*, 1967, *20*, p. 1106.
9　E. Fabricius, 'Crucial Periods in the Development of the Following Response in Young Nidifugous Birds', *Acta Psychol.*, 1964, *23*, pp. 100–101.
10　P. Guiton, 'The Effect of Isolation on the Following Response of Brown Leghorn Chicks', *Proc. Roy. Phys. Soc. Edinb.*, 1958, *27*, pp. 9–14.
11　W. Sluckin and E. A. Salzen, 'Imprinting and Perceptual Learning', *Quart. J. Exp. Psychol.*, 1961, *13*, pp. 65–77.
12　D. Asdourian, 'Object Attachment and the Critical Period', *Psychonom. Sci.*, 1967, *7*, pp. 235–236.
13　P. Guiton, 'Socialization and Imprinting in Brown Leghorn Chicks', *Anim. Behav.*, 1959, *7*, pp. 26–34.
14　A. Baron and G. B. Kish, 'Early Social Isolation as a Determinant of Aggregative Behavior in the Domestic Chicken', *J. Comp. Physiol. Psychol.*, 1960, *53*, pp. 459–463.
15　A. Baron, G. B. Kish and J. J. Antonitis, 'Stimulus Determinants

of Aggregative Behaviour in the Domestic Chicken', *J. Genet. Psychol.*, 1961, *98*, pp. 177–182.

16 E. Williams and J. P. Scott, 'The Development of Social Behavior Patterns in the Mouse, in Relation to Natural Periods', *Behaviour*, 1953, *6*, pp. 35–64.

17 J. P. Scott, 'Critical Periods in the Development of Social Behavior in Puppies', *Psychosom. Med.*, 1958, *20*, pp. 42–54.

18 J. P. Scott, 'Critical Periods in Behavioural Development', *Science*, 1962, *138*, pp. 949–958.

19 J. L. Fuller and L. D. Clark, 'Genetic and Treatment Factors Modifying the Postisolation Syndrome in Dogs', *J. Comp. Physiol. Psychol.*, 1966, *61*, pp. 251–257.

20 T. C. Schneirla and J. S. Rosenblatt, ' "Critical Periods" in the Development of Behavior', *Science*, 1963, *139*, pp. 1110–1115.

21 H. F. Harlow and M. K. Harlow, 'Social Deprivation in Monkeys', *Sci. Amer.*, 1962, *207*, pp. 137–146.

22 C. B. Stendler, 'Critical Periods in Socialization and Over-dependency', *Child Devel.*, 1952, *23*, pp. 3–12.

23 J. P. Scott, 'The Process of Primary Socialization in Canine and Human Infants', *Monogr. Soc. Res. Child Devel.*, 1963, *28*, No. 1, pp. 1–47.

24 J. A. Ambrose, 'The Concept of Critical Period for the Development of Social Responsiveness in Early Human Infancy', in *Determinants of Infant Behaviour*, *II*, ed. B. M. Foss, 1963, London: Methuen.

25 V. H. Denenberg, 'Critical Periods, Stimulus Input, and Emotional Reactivity', *Psychol. Rev.*, 1964, *71*, pp. 335–351.

CHAPTER 7

Imitation

In earlier chapters we considered typical conditioning and imprinting in infancy, as well as certain kinds of early experience which may be marginally regarded as early learning. We have not yet looked at learning by imitation which can occur early in life, nor at some learning situations characteristic of human beings, as distinct from animals, such as language acquisition. This chapter is concerned with early imitative learning in animals and man, and the next – with early human language learning.

Imitation involves two individuals: a subject or *observer* who imitates and a *model* who is imitated. Imitation is said to have occurred when the subject's behaviour is more similar to the model's behaviour than it would have been had the subject not observed the model. At this point one could introduce some distinctions which would perhaps suggest that the word imitation refers to a number of distinguishable processes. The situation is further complicated by the fact that various terms other than imitation have been used with reference to some of the phenomena which come under the global definition of imitation given above. The various terms in use, and some types of imitation, are surveyed in a later section of this chapter.

The reader will see that, along with some other writers, we use the word imitation as a broad, generic term. However, it may be helpful to note that some employ this word in a more restricted way. Thus, it could be said that when the observer imitates the model only after a considerable time interval, then we are concerned not with imitation but with observational learning. In fact, one could regard observational learning either as different from imitation or as a sub-species of imitation; and some writers – as a matter of fact – have used the term, observational learning, as synonymous with imitation.

However this may be, we must at the outset also draw attention to another problem. Imitation in so far as it refers to the occurrence of matching responses may or may not involve learning. On the whole, if the responses acquired by the observer are new, if the observer has not made them before, then learning would have occurred. But apart from the occurrence of matching behaviour there is the question of the origin of the tendency to produce matching responses. One may ask whether this tendency is essentially innate or learned. We shall return to this in our survey of findings of early initiative behaviour.

It appears that imitation cannot take place before the organism has reached a certain level of perceptual development. While it does sometimes occur relatively early in life, no form of imitation appears to be common in very early infancy. And yet imitation seems to play a part in the acquisition of quite basic modes of behaviour, including in some animal species the learning of 'feeding habits, aversions and social expectations'. (1) There is little doubt that in young children a great deal of ordinary, every-day behaviour emerges as a developmental sequence of the different phenomena subsumed under imitation. (2, 3)

I.   Social facilitation and observational learning in young animals

Sometimes an animal in the presence of a companion will start acting like the companion. It is well known, for instance, that a seemingly satiated animal may start eating again when its hungry companion, acting as a model, does so. Sometimes the companion's behaviour has this facilitatory effect, and on occasions his mere presence may bring about some action on the part of the subject. Such facilitation has been observed in both mature and young animals.

The social facilitation of feeding behaviour has been systematically studied in the domestic chick. (4, 5) It was established in several experiments that complete social contact is a necessary condition of increase in food consumption, and that somehow chicks are led to 'eat more through pecking of one another's bills'. The longer the subject is deprived of food the more it is susceptible to social facilitation. Furthermore, the longer the companion is food-deprived, the more the subject, too, will eat. Tapping a pencil on the floor near food in the presence of a chick has been found to make the chick eat more.

Such social facilitation of feeding may or may not be imitation in the every-day sense of the word. At any rate, it represents some acquisition of behaviour by the young chick. The modification of behaviour appears to be elicited by the pecking of companions, or by stimulation such as pencil tapping, and the like. Apparently no prior learning is needed for a social facilitation of feeding to occur. (4) J. P. Scott has gathered together evidence of social facilitation in the dog. (6) In addition to eating, running may be brought about by the running of the companion animal. And in other animals, birds and mammals, various complex activities, such as nest-building, may be the result of imitation or social facilitation.

While social facilitation of feeding occurs in the chick without any prior training, there is some evidence from the study of adult animals in various contexts that some kind of early social experience is helpful, if not essential, for the development of socially facilitated modes of behaviour. (7) However, there will continue to be uncertainty about the generality of this until much more research into the different aspects of the problem has been done.

Vocal imitation in birds is common enough, but the imitation by the young of some species of the song of the mature fellow-members of the species has some special features. One is that such learning by imitation occurs only during the first few months of life; it is irreversible in that it is never forgotten and is exclusive in that no other song can subsequently be learned. For these reasons some students of animal behaviour look upon this type of initial imitative learning as akin to imprinting. (8)

Many observations of early song-learning in birds have been reported by W. H. Thorpe who had himself conducted extensive studies of the chaffinch. (8) Obviously, bird songs cannot be readily described in words, but their spectrographic records can nowadays be analysed and compared with one another. (9) While some birds imitate complete songs of other species, the chaffinch is very selective, restricting itself to the learning of song from conspecifics. The birds learn only when they are immature, before they are themselves able to produce a full song, which is before their first Spring of life. Those kept out of hearing of all bird song develop a very simple song pattern which noticeably differs from that of the normal chaffinch. To some extent such learning occurs also in certain other species, notably the blackbird and the meadowlark. (10)

Imitation in mammals, let alone imitation in them early in life, had at one time been seriously in doubt, despite the common notion of 'aping'. However, evidence of observational learning in various species is now quite conclusive. The introduction of the so-called duplicate cage method of study, (11) whereby both the untrained observer animal and the trained model are coping with identical tasks in separate adjacent cages, has helped a great deal to show what animals will do when given the opportunity to learn observationally. K. R. L. Hall assembled all existing developmental studies of observational learning in monkeys and apes. (12) Many of them are probably not wholly reliable, but taken together they indicate that observational learning in infancy plays a significant part in determining behaviour patterns in the adult life of many primate species.

It remains yet to be established whether observational learning is influential in the long run only when it occurs during the more sensitive periods of the behavioural ontogeny. There is some evidence that feeding habits, and other likes and dislikes, are acquired early in life by young monkeys in zoos and in the wild. And imitation, almost human in character, has been observed in the chimpanzee. (13) But there is need for much more research into the role of imitation in the learning of the young of different mammalian species. Two separate lines of research should be pursued: first, how much is actually learned by imitation or observationally, and second, how much of the imitative behaviour itself is learned. As hinted at earlier, the distinction between the two is that between imitative learning on the one hand and learning to learn imitatively, on the other. Our knowledge of early learning of both kinds is as yet anything but extensive.

II.   *Imitative behaviour in children*

Human infants begin to show signs of imitation at perhaps about one month of age. These signs are initially barely discernible, but phenomena such as 'contagious crying' may soon be observed. Actual imitation of actions of other people and of sounds uttered by others comes only later. Piaget has described the stages of this development. (2) At about four months, the infant appears to begin to match actions of other people, e.g. hand-clapping, with his own actions; and later, likewise, the child attempts to imitate sounds. Such matching of the behaviour of models appears to result in a great deal of learning at the age of about one year. When the child, instead of imitating immediately, begins to be able to defer imitative action for some time, then learning mediated by representational thinking may be said to have set in.

A very considerable number of experiments aiming at elucidating imitative behaviour in children have been conducted in several laboratories since about 1960. Earlier work was reviewed by Bandura and Walters. (14) These writers have also been largely instrumental in initiating and stimulating the more recent research work of which there is now a comprehensive review by Flanders. (15) The existing studies have been concerned with the role of reinforcement in imitation, the effects of different training and incentive conditions, the influence of the characteristics of the model, and so forth. They have been for the most part studies of children rather than infants; and they have not on the whole been developmental in conception. Thus experiments on imitative behaviour in children do not readily come under the heading of early learning. However, it would be highly desirable to broaden the study of initial learning by further investigating experimentally in young children the onset and development of learning by imitation.

III.   *Terminology*

So far we have used the terms imitation, social facilitation and observational learning sufficiently loosely to enable us to by-pass the problem of specifying and clarifying these and related concepts. While not essential for empirical research, there are never-theless distinct advantages in attempting some conceptual clarification in a field where the nature of the research itself may be influenced by the ideas we have about what it is that we are setting out to study. Our aim now, however, is less ambitious; it is simply to mention the different terms used in this field and to consider what they mean to the various writers who have used them.

J. P. Scott has drawn attention to the distinction between social facilitation and alleeomimetic behaviour. The latter is concerned with flocking in birds, schooling in fishes, etc., whereby a number of individuals act alike at the same time. Thus allelomimesis refers 'to a particular kind of behaviour, whereas social facilitation is a positive *change* in any kind of behaviour', (6) and both situations might be described as imitative. Flocking and similar types of behaviour have, of course, also to do with mutual approach and following, and possibly, imprinting. Social facilitation refers, on the other hand, to feeding and generally to actions other than approach responses.

Some writers take, however, a rather broader view of social facilitation. They consider under this heading *all* situations in which the action of an individual is influenced by what others do. Such a broad connotation of the term 'social facilitation' suggests that other related terms, such as 'imitation', allelomimesis', and several others mentioned below, might be best regarded as sub-classes of 'social facilitation'. (16)

While it is largely a matter of accepted usage of language how social facilitation is related to such terms as, for example, 'identification' or 'vicarious learning', there is little doubt that the so-called behavioural contagion is a form of social facilitation. Students of animal behaviour have noticed that both in zoos and in the wild eccentric feeding ways spread among members of a group of animals. (17) Likewise when, for instance, yawning or laughing spreads among a crowd of people, the particular behaviour in question may be described as contagious.

The social facilitation of emotion in human beings, whereby the observer imitates the affect of the model, is said to be an essential feature of the process known as empathy. (18) In this the observer wholly identifies with the model, although the term 'identification' is clearly broader than 'empathy'. For it may be said – though this is a controversial issue – that identification refers to cases where the person 'takes on' the feeling and overt behaviour of another, acting as if he or she were that other person. An analysis of usages of the word 'identification' in ordinary speech would reveal that in some contexts identification has little to do with imitation while in others the distinction between it and 'imitation' is largely blurred.

In every-day speech 'imitation' certainly means 'copying the behaviour of others'. And, as we have seen, observational learning may mean copying after some delay, although some writers prefer to use the term 'observational learning' simply as a substitute for imitation (which, because of its supposed theoretical implications, could be misleading). (12) Observational learning is learning by watching rather than by trying. It is therefore sometimes termed 'vicarious learning'. While the model may be laboriously learning something by trial and error, the observer in suitable circumstances will learn the same task vicariously. The observer may thus learn something without a single trial; hence vicarious learning is also known as no-trial learning. And because the learner's behaviour matches that of the model, such learning has been called matched-dependent behaviour. (19)

The multitude of terms used is perhaps a testimony to the importance of imitation phenomena in daily life. It also suggests that subtle differences exist in the operation of imitation in various situations. These differences may be specified quite precisely, and suitable labels may be given to operationally different types of imitation. (20) A factor that contributes to the multiplicity of terms in use is that the different theoretical approaches to imitation are bound up with traditionally different phraseologies. Thus the concept of identification is associated with the Freudian view, matched-dependent behaviour – with the Miller/Dollard approach, and so on. And it must be recognized that is is difficult to study imitative behaviour both in mature individuals and in the young without some reference to theories of imitation.

IV.   *Theoretical approaches to imitation*

It might be argued that the different behavioural contingencies to which the term 'imitation' may be applied differ so greatly from one another that it would be misleading to regard them as belonging to one class of phenomena; in other words, there may not be any such single entity as imitation. (21) Whether or not this type of view is tenable, the word 'imitation' is a useful descriptive term, whatever, if any, its explanatory value. At one time some writers tended to regard the potential to imitate as innate, (22) while others believed it to be acquirable through learning. (19) It is now widely recognized that both genetic make-up and learning may combine to determine the individual's general ability to imitate.

As indicated earlier, the challenging problems concerning imitation have been (a) to what extent imitative behaviour in general is acquired, (b) how, exactly, general imitative ability may be acquired, and (c) how anything specific learned by imitation is learned. There has been no dearth of theorizing, and the problems and theories have been reviewed and evaluated in recent years in a number of papers. (15, 23, 24, 25) Some early approaches attempted to explain imitation in terms of classical conditioning, while another type of explanation stemmed from the Freudian view of the mechanism of identification. Most theories, old and new, have been partly concerned with the onset of imitative behaviour, and so have implications for the study of early learning.

An influential approach to imitation was put forward by Miller and Dollard. (19) It asserts that imitative behaviour depends on the individual's prior discrimination learning coupled with a high-drive state at the time of the actual imitation. Everything turns on the character of the earlier discrimination learning. The theory suggests that this has involved a reduction of drive whenever the observer's response happened to be similar to the model's response. In other words, prior instrumental conditioning of certain responses, and not an innate tendency to imitate, would account for what the subject has learned to do. There have been other interesting theoretical developments in the learning-theory tradition. (18, 26) An important implication for early learning of at least some explanations in terms of learning theory is that the human infant is assumed to be 'practising covertly the characteristic actions of other people with whom he interacts'. (27) However, it is difficult to see how empirical studies to check such suggestions can be conducted.

The more recent theoretical formulations by Bandura and his

colleagues propose that imitation involves a learning by contiguity of certain stimulus sequences in the course of watching a model, and that the recall of these sequences in some manner guides the observer in his later behaviour. (28) This would appear to be exposure learning of stimulus sequences rather than exposure learning of the characteristics of stimuli, as in imprinting. Thus, in the first place, response potential is changed without any actual change of performance. Subsequently, through the influence of reinforcing conditions, the performance itself begins to change, and imitative action is achieved. Whether such hypothesizing about imitation can initiate worthwhile empirical investigations of early imitative learning in infants remains to be seen.

NOTES

1 K. R. L. Hall, 'Imitative Learning as a Factor in the Development of Monkey and Ape Behaviour', *Bull. Br. Psychol. Soc.*, 1962, No. 47, A8–A9.
2 J. Piaget, *Play, Dreams, and Imitation in Childhood*, 1951, London: Norton.
3 A. Bandura, 'Social Learning through Imitation', in *Nebraska Symposium on Motivation*, ed. M. S. Jones, 1962, Lincoln: University of Nebraska Press.
4 C. W. Tolman, 'Social Facilitation of Feeding Behaviour in the Domestic Chick, *Anim. Behav.*, 1964, *12*, pp. 245–251.
5 C. W. Tolman and G. F. Wilson, 'Social Feeding in Domestic Chicks', *Anim. Behav.*, 1965, *13*, pp. 134–142.
6 J. P. Scott, 'Social Facilitation and Allelomimetic Behavior', in *Social Facilitation and Imitative Behavior*, eds. E. C. Simmel, R. A. Hoppe and G. A. Milton, 1968, Boston: Allyn and Bacon.
7 C. W. Tolman, 'The Role of the Companion in Social Facilitation of Animal Behavior', in *Social Facilitation and Imitative Behavior*, eds. E. C. Simmel, R. A. Hoppe and G. A. Milton, 1968. Boston: Allyn and Bacon.
8 W. H. Thorpe, *Learning and Instinct in Animals*, 1963, London: Methuen.
9 W. H. Thorpe, 'The Process of Song-learning in the Chaffinch as Studied by Means of the Sound Spectrograph', *Nature*, 1954, *173*, pp. 465.
10 R. A. Hinde, *Animal Behaviour: A Synthesis of Ethology and Comparative Psychology*, 1966, New York and London: McGraw-Hill.

11 C. J. Warden and T. A. Jackson, 'Imitative Behaviour in the Rhesus Monkey', *J. Genet. Psychol.*, 1935, *46*, pp. 103–125.

12 K. R. L. Hall, 'Observational Learning in Monkeys and Apes', *Br. J. Psychol.*, 1963, *54*, pp. 201–226.

13 K. J. Hayes and C. Hayes, 'Imitation in a Home-raised Chimpanzee', *J. Comp. Physiol. Psychol.*, 1952, *45*, pp. 450–459.

14 A. Bandura and R. H. Walters, *Social Learning and Personality Development*, 1963, New York: Holt.

15 J. P. Flanders, 'A Review of Research on Imitative Behaviour', *Psychol. Bull.*, 1968, *69*, pp. 316–337.

16 G. A. Milton, Introductory Note, in *Social Facilitation and Imitative Behavior*, eds. E. C. Simmel, R. A. Hoppe and G. A. Milton, 1968, Boston: Allyn and Bacon.

17 H. Hediger, *Wild Animals in Captivity*, 1950, London: Butterworth.

18 O. H. Mowrer, *Learning Theory and the Symbolic Processes*, 1960, New York: Wiley.

19 N. E. Miller and J. Dollard, *Social Learning and Imitation*, 1941, New Haven: Yale University Press.

20 D. S. Wright, Personal communication. See also D. S. Wright et al,. *Introducing Psychology*, 1970, Ch. 21, Harmondsworth, Middlesex: Penguin Books.

21 H. W. Nissen, 'Social Behavior in Primates', in *Comparative Psychology*, ed. C. P. Stone, 1951, New York: Prentice-Hall.

22 W. McDougall, *Introduction to Social Psychology*, 1908, London: Methuen.

23 A. Bandura, 'Vicarious Processes: a Case of No-trial Learning', in *Advances in Experimental Social Psychology*, 1965, Vol. 2., ed. L. Berkowitz, New York: Academic Press.

24 B. M. Foss, 'Imitation', in *Determinants of Infant Behaviour, III*, ed. B. M. Foss, 1965, London: Methuen.

25 J. B. Gilmore, 'Toward an Understanding of Imitation', in *Social Facilitation and Imitative Behavior*, eds. E. C. Simmel, R. A. Hoppe and G. A. Milton, 1968, Boston: Allyn and Bacon.

26 J. L. Gewirtz and K. G. Stingle, 'Learning of Generalized Imitation as the Basis for Identification', *Psychol. Rev.*, 1968, *75*, pp. 374–397.

27 Eleanor E. Maccoby, 'Role-taking in Childhood and its Consequences for Social Learning', *Child Devel.*, 1959, *30*, pp. 239–252.

28 A. Bandura, 'Social Learning Theory of Identificatory Processes', in *Handbook of Socialization Theory and Research*, ed. D. A. Goslin, 1968, Chicago: Rand-McNally.

CHAPTER 8

The Beginnings of Language

It is commonplace that imitation plays a part in the infant's early learning of language; the problem is to clarify and to specify this part, or so it might appear. But, as we have seen, the elucidation of imitation is itself a problem not susceptible to a quick and easy solution. Therefore, at the present time any attempt to explain language acquisition simply in terms of imitation would be jejune. It could also be, and has been, said that the infant is conditioned to acquire speech. If this is the case, then the scientist's task would be to demonstrate what *precisely* goes on in such conditioning. In fact, several different views have been expressed as to *how* a young child learns to speak. The actual, empirical studies of language acquisition seem to stem directly from the extant theories. Now it is relatively easy to survey studies of early conditioning, or of imprinting, or even of imitation, without necessarily placing them in one or another theoretical framework. Not so – with the beginnings of language; here theory dominates research.

I. *Early learning to speak*

Communication by means of symbols in terms of gestures and words is a peculiarly human characteristic. The ability to communicate verbally is acquired by the infant quite rapidly, between the ages of approximately one and a half and three and a half years. Attempts have been made to study the development of language experimentally, varying systematically the conditions of verbal stimulation to which the young child is exposed. (1) However, such research is in its infancy; and our ideas about the character of language learning in young children are mainly based on a combination of observational studies and theorizing.

The interest in language development is an old one. D. A. McCarthy surveyed earlier studies of the development of gestures and speech, and reported on the state of knowledge a good many years ago. (2) The obvious role of imitation in the growth of vocabulary has been stressed. Russian workers had been interested for a long time in the acquisition of grammatical speech. American learning theorists in the behaviourist tradition had implied that language learning, like any other learning, was – in principle – analysable in terms of stimulus-response conditioning; and this view has found its way into many standard text-books of psychology. However, investigations of the acquisition of vocabulary and manifest grammar, and some traditional explanations of how a child learns to speak, suffer perhaps from an initial weakness. That weakness is inherent in the formulations of the problem or object of study.

In more recent years students of linguistics have begun to ask what precisely it is that the infant acquires in learning to speak. One answer which has been given is that to have learned a language is to have learned to make speech transformations. (3, 4) This may involve understanding that two sentences with totally different structures can have the same meaning, or realizing that a given sentence can have two meanings, or saying something intelligible that has never been heard before, and so on. Speech transformations are made according to certain rules implicit in the language, which he who has learned to speak appears to know intuitively and can apply to new situations, without being fully aware what he does and how he does it. This acquired knowledge of transformational rules enables the speaker to wield the language flexibly and creatively. Thus, according to many modern students of linguistics, the essential feature of language acquisition is the acquisition of the so-called transformational grammar. The latter may be inferred like ordinary grammar, though less directly, from modes of speaking adopted by the native speakers of any language. And in explaining how language is learned by a young child a theory must be capable of explaining how the command of transformational grammar is acquired.

II. *Different types of theoretical approach*

The situation concerning the study of the beginnings of language in infants may be described as one of quite extensive but very patchy knowledge of developmental stages coupled with uncertainty about the combination of factors governing the progress of speech acquisition. This is a good breeding ground for the springing up of rival theories. At the present time there are two or three main types of theory offering to explain how the native language is learned. (4, 5) At the one extreme there are traditional learning-theory accounts, explaining language acquisition in terms of operant conditioning, or of mediated stimulus-response connections, or of contextual generalization, or something to that effect. At the other extreme are the frankly nativist accounts, that is those that postulate the operation of some built-in language-acquisition mechanism, universal in the human species, which makes it possible for any language to be learned in infancy quickly and efficiently. In addition, an intermediate type of theory upholds the importance of gradual learning, but not primarily of learning which can be adequately described in terms of traditional conditioning procedures.

III. *Operant learning*

A point of view about learning to talk, consistent with the operant-conditioning account of learning, has been forcefully put forward by Skinner. (6) According to this, any element of behaviour – verbal or otherwise – is strengthened and maintained when it is systematically followed by reinforcement. The infant's initial repertoire of sounds may be small, but from the beginning the parent, knowingly or unwittingly, reinforces some utterances and not others. Thereafter the infant's verbal behaviour is suitably shaped up by the reinforcement of only those verbal responses which get closer and closer to what is desired by the adult interacting with the infant.

Thus acquiring a language would appear to consist of a gradual 'natural selection' of sounds. Natural variations or mutations in utterances are exploited so that the infant's babbling undergoes an evolution which terminates in speech resembling that of the infant's parents. Even after language has been acquired reinforcing consequences of the child's verbal responses continue to be important; for, if extinction is not to set in, the strength of these responses must be kept up. The role of prior stimuli is said to be as crucial in verbal behaviour as in any other. Discrimination learning by the infant ensures that what he says is relevant to the signal stimulus he receives. Skinner gives many examples of how speech comes about, or could come about. It is difficult to deny the role of operant conditioning in the process of learning to talk. But many find it equally difficult to believe that language acquisition – and particularly the acquisition of transformational grammar – can be adequately accounted for along Skinnerian lines.

IV. *Other traditional-type accounts*

O. H. Mowrer has been particularly concerned with the pre-verbal beginnings of language. (7) The infant is taken to associate the mother's voice and utterances with need-satisfying circumstances. When the infant hears his own randomly generated babbling, he tends to repeat those sounds that are like the ones previously heard from the mother and other people under conditions of his own need-reduction. The child's pleasure is, thus, in the first place his own somatic response to need-reduction; it then becomes attached to particular human sounds, and finally the pleasure response becomes a response to his own vocalizations. The mother then further reinforces these vocalizations, which are like her own sounds, and so the child learns that imitation of her speech pays; in this way, then, the language of the adults around the infant is gradually acquired by him through appropriate imitation.

Although this type of view has been under severe attack for some years it has certainly not been universally abandoned. On the contrary, it has recently been put forward in a new form with renewed force. (8) Thus, A. W. Staats reiterates the belief that classical and instrumental conditioning principles are 'the basic laws' of learning, including language learning. Speech sounds – initially neutral stimuli – are made by parents and others as the infant is being cared for, that is, as positive reinforcers (food, etc.)

are provided and negative ones (discomfort, etc.) are removed. In this way speech sounds 'become positive learned (or conditioned) reinforcers'. Furthermore, the more the child's own speech is like the speech of others the more reinforcing it will be. These are the rudiments of the view of language learning which is consistent with the behaviourist tradition.

However, because using language has manifestly something to do with thinking, theories have been put forward which, although in the behaviourist stimulus-response tradition, give a more sophisticated account of language acquisition. One such appears to stem from the so-called mediational account of thought processes, (9) and bases language development on mediated S–R connections. Another theory offers an explanation of language acquisition which suggests that the ability to grasp grammar depends on a continuous operation of contextual generalization; that is, the child learns the position of a word or phrase in the context of one sentence, and generalizes this to other sentences. Here, then, is a special case of a combination of ordinary stimulus generalization and response generalization which – is is said – provides the basis for linguistic creativity. However, all extensions of learning theory to the realm of language have been repeatedly and severely criticized on the ground that they simply cannot give an account of the acquisition of transformational grammar, or simply, that they do not properly fit the known facts about learning to talk; (4) and these facts basically are that the infant learns fast, that he needs relatively little practice at talking, and that he soon uses language in a constructive manner.

V.   Non-traditional views

A strictly nativist approach would be entirely unconstructive. To say that an infant is endowed with an 'innate capacity for language' is to say something that is in one sense obvious and, in another, untestable. It is clear that human beings can learn languages; but the view that they have the capacity to acquire syntax, and 'feel' for structuring sentences, without some relevant learning, is not susceptible to further study. Thus, it is easier to deny that a traditional learning view, even when elaborately refined and embellished, is incapable of explaining how the ability to speak a language is acquired than to put forward any alternative account. Still, the denial itself can have seeds of constructive suggestions; and some students of linguistics and some psychologists have put forward critiques of S–R theorizing along with some nativistically orientated theoretical proposals. (10, 11)

The proponents of this type of approach maintain in the first place that the understanding and producing of sentences does not depend on 'probability learning'; and secondly that 'babbling, hearing oneself talk, and imitation are neither sufficient nor necessary factors in the acquisition of grammar'; (12) and the latter statement can be well backed up with clinical observations.

Thus, some studies show that there are patients in whom initial organic defects have prevented the making of sounds necessary for speech; and yet, although these persons have not acquired the ability to speak, they behave in a way which indicates that they understand language. One such case has been described in detail, (13) and it suggests that it is not at all necessary for the young child to hear itself speak in order to learn the grammatical structure of the language. And further, there are also observations of those mental defectives (mongols) who do make the full range of speech sounds, and who do imitate, but who never fully acquire grammar. The verbal behaviour of these children simply cannot be shaped into grammatical language. Therefore, it looks as if the learning of language requires the capacity for attaining comprehension which is just not present in these particular mentally defective persons.

Partly as a result of such findings, some workers in the field of psycholinguistics look in favour upon the concept of 'biologically given capacities' inherent in human beings for acquiring language early in life. (13) There is a suggestion of the 'language acquisition device' within us all which provides the necessary basis for language learning. (10) Some psycholinguists appear to believe that exposure to language is sufficient for the acquisition of it, in the way that visual exposure to a figure determines the young animal's imprinted attachment to that figure. Even so, there is at present no satisfactory theory, which is in principle testable, to account for the rapid learning not only of words and phrases but also of linguistic rules which are the essence of the knowledge of language. (14)

The current attempts at theory-building range from those that propose a great deal by way of detailed content within the built-in 'language acquisition device' to those that assume the child to be born not so much with a set of linguistic categories as with a mechanism for processing linguistic data. (15, 16) The latter view implies that the main problem of developmental psycholinguistics is to discover the precise nature of the learning process in language acquisition, rather than dogmatize as to what is innate.

In this vein many workers stress the importance of learning, albeit not conditioning in the usual sense of the term. Roger Brown and co-workers suggest, for instance, that, far from learning by imitation, the child 'induces' general rules implicit in the language he hears, and that it is the acquisition of this knowledge which enables him to make proper use of the language, generating sentences never previously heard. (17, 18) As a general statement this may be unexceptionable; however, current theory-building grapples with the problem of specifying the details of these processes.

The precise role of imitation is as yet unclear. Slobin, whose approach is broadly of a similar type to that of McNeill, or Brown, argues that imitation 'is certainly not necessary in learning to understand, nor does it ensure learning to speak'. And yet imitation, whatever the role of reinforcement, appears to play a part in the early acquisition of the rules of language. (19) It would seem that rule-learning theories of language acquisition may provide new suggestions for specific empirical studies, both observational and experimental, and thus eventually clarify the character of the earliest learning of language.

VI. *Some empirical findings*

It has been clear for a long time that the young child shows some understanding of language before he can actually speak, (2) and it has more recently been clinically established that the ability to speak is not at all a necessary condition for comprehension. (12) The question may be asked whether understanding normally precedes speech production in children who already do speak a little and are learning to speak more and better. This is where laboratory experimentation can help. In one ingenious study 12 three-year-old children were tested on a number of grammatical contrasts. (20) Understanding was operationally defined as 'the correct understanding of pictures named by contrasting sentences'. Production was defined in two ways, (*i*) as 'the correct imitation of contrasting features in sentences without evidence of understanding', and (*ii*) as 'the correct production of contrasting features in sentences applied appropriately to pictures'. Speech production in the latter sense was found to be less advanced than sheer understanding, though parrot-like imitation was possible well before understanding.

Other systematic studies of the beginnings of language in young children have revealed the function of the adults, usually parents, in the child's language development. Somewhat surprisingly, a common feature of the child-parent dialogue is the parent's imitation of what the child says. However, such imitation is not fully accurate, in that the parent's response often consists of repeating what the child says in an amplified and modified form. (17) Thus, the child's utterance is 'expanded' into a well-formed sentence. The parents – it is reported – treat in this manner about one-third of what two-year-old infants say. And the infant benefits from such expansions by adopting later the constructions produced by the parent.

The stages in the acquisition of syntax and morphology have been rather more extensively studied in Russian than in English. (21) In recent years the early syntax of English-speaking children has begun to be investigated. (18, 22) A feature of early speech is that a small number of 'pivot' words can each combine with any of the words within a large open class into two-word sentences. A study of children's speech development in Japan suggests that the acquisition of basic grammatical relations follows the same pattern in Japanese as in Indo-European languages. (15, 23) A good many other detailed findings could be quoted; what is interesting is that generally what is studied, and what is found, seems to depend greatly on the theoretical orientation of the research worker. The really important question for the student of early learning is how the beginnings of language compare with the beginnings of other skills. Despite the different (and conflicting) affirmative proposals found in the literature, the answer to this question cannot as yet be said to be known.

NOTES

1 C. B. Cazden, 'Some Implications of Research on Language Development for Pre-school Education', in *Early Education*, eds. R. D. Hess and R. M. Bear, 1968, Chicago: Aldine.

2 D. A. McCarthy, 'Language Development in Children', in *Manual of Child Psychology*, ed. L. Carmichael, 1954, New York: Wiley.

3 N. Chomsky, 'Current Issues in Linguistic Theory', in *The Structure of Language*, eds. J. A. Fodor and J. J. Katz, 1964, Englewood Cliffs, N.J.: Prentice-Hall.

4 D. McNeill, 'On Theories of Language Acquisition', in *Verbal Behavior and General Behavior Theory*, eds. T. R. Dixon and D. L. Horton, 1968, Englewood Cliffs, N.J.: Prentice-Hall.

5 N. S. Endler, L. R. Boulter and H. Osser, *Contemporary Issues in Developmental Psychology*, 1968, New York: Holt, Rinehart and Winston

6 B. F. Skinner, *Verbal Behavior*, 1957, New York: Appleton.

7 O. H. Mowrer, *Learning Theory and Symbolic Processes*, 1960, New York: Wiley.

8 A. W. Staats, *Learning, Language and Cognition*, 1968, New York: Holt, Rinehart and Winston.

9 C. E. Osgood, G. J. Suci and P. H. Tannenbaum, *The Measurement of Meaning*, 1957, Urbana: University of Illinois Press.

10 N. Chomsky, *Aspects of the Theory of Syntax*, 1965, Cambridge, Mass.: M.I.T. Press.

11 E. H. Lenneberg, 'A Biological Perspective of Language', in *New Directions in the Study of Language*, ed. E. H. Lenneberg, 1964, Cambridge, Mass.: M.I.T. Press.

12 E. H. Lenneberg, 'Understanding Language Without Ability to Speak: a Case Report', *J. Abn. Soc. Psychol.*, 1962, *65*, pp. 419–425.

13 E. H. Lenneberg, *Biological Foundations of Language*, 1967, New York: Wiley.

14 E. Ingram, 'Recent Trends in Psycholinguistics', *Br. J. Psychol.*, 1968, *59*, pp. 315–325.

15 D. McNeill, 'Developmental Psycholinguistics', in *The Genesis of Language*, eds. F. Smith and G. A. Miller, 1966, Cambridge, Mass.: M.I.T. Press.

16 D. I. Slobin, 'Comments on "Developmental Psycholinguistics",' in *The Genesis of Language*, eds. F. Smith and G. A. Miller, 1966, Cambridge, Mass.: M.I.T. Press.

17 R. Brown and U. Bellugi, 'Three Processes in the Child's Acquisition of Syntax', *Harvard Educ. Rev.*, 1964, *34*, pp. 133–151.

18 R. Brown and C. Fraser, 'The Acquisition of Syntax', *Monogr. Soc. Res. Child Developm.*, 1964, *29*, pp. 43–79.

19 D. I. Slobin, 'Imitation and Grammatical Development in Children', in *Contemporary Issues in Developmental Psychology*, eds. N. S. Endler, L. R. Boulter and H. Osser, 1968, New York: Holt, Rinehart and Winston.

20 C. Fraser, U. Bellugi and R. Brown, 'Control of Grammar in Imitation, Comprehension and Production', *J. Verb. Lear. Verb. Behav.*, 1963, *2*, pp. 121–135.

21 D. I. Slobin, 'The Acquisition of Russian as a Native Language', in *The Genesis of Language*, eds. F. Smith and G. A. Miller, 1966, Cambridge, Mass.: M.I.T. Press.

22 M. D. S. Braine, 'The Ontogeny of English Phrase Structure: the First Phrase', *Language*, 1963, *39*, pp. 1–13.

23 D. McNeill, 'The Creation of Language by Children', in *Psycholinguistic Papers*, eds. J. Lyons and R. J. Wales, 1966, Edinburgh: Edinburgh University Press.

CHAPTER 9

The Emergence of Individuality

Each individual, animal or human, has a unique genetic potential. Likewise his environment, strictly speaking, is unlike any other. Heredity and environment combine to determine both the physical and behavioural characteristics of the individual. Thus, the determinants of behaviour, but not the behaviour itself, may be classified into hereditary and environmental. Behaviour as such is always a function of both sets of factors. Nevertheless a distinction is often made between innate and learned modes of behaviour. Is this distinction misleading?

Those who uphold the concept of innate behaviour do so because of the results of the so-called 'deprivation experiment' in which animals react to certain stimulus configurations in a stereotyped fashion, even when deprived of what might have been thought to be relevant experience. (1) Such behaviour would be defined as innate in a negative manner, namely that it requires no learning. But what cannot be shown to require learning is not, in principle, independent of experience. For the 'information' carried by genes can only be realized in structure, as well as in behaviour, through the interaction of the organism with its environment. In other words, the appearance of all responses in the course of development depends on both nature and nurture, and attempts at assigning responses to one or the other source are unrealistic. (2)

Nevertheless the phrase 'innate behaviour' may be useful when it is used to refer to behaviour that is scarcely influenced by variations of environment. In such circumstances innate behaviour would be taken to mean *environmentally stable* behaviour. Such stability is a matter of degree; and behaviour that is markedly influenced in its development by environmental variations could be described as *environmentally labile*. (3) In the development of this type of behaviour early learning looms large. This chapter is concerned with the role of early learning in the crystallization of individuality in man and animal.

I. *Personality development and learning*

An understanding of the unequeness of the individual rests on the study of individual differences. As far as human beings are concerned this is what the topic of personality is about. Descriptions of personality are in terms of types, traits, factors, etc., whereby personality characteristics and differences arc expressed quantatively. Theories of personality set out to explain the causes of the individual differences. No single one of the many theories is generally accepted; and there is some difficulty in finding suitable criteria by which to judge how good any particular theory is.

Research in the field of personality determinants is influenced in its direction and scope by personality theories. However, the research findings make a body of empirical knowledge which stands largely on its own feet and does not fit snugly into any theoretical framework. The determinants of human personality include, of course, early childhood experiences; and our special concern is that range of experiences in infancy which may be regarded as learning. Very broadly, this involves the acquisition of parental attitudes which results from the specific child-parent relations and the influences of the family environment in general; and it also includes much learning which is the direct result of the child-training practices adopted by the parents. A great deal of early learning leads to socialization. But socialization itself has been defined as the outcome of the processes 'whereby an individual acquires his personality, motives, values, attitudes, opinions, standards and beliefs'. (4)

Granted the genetic and the intra-uterine environmental influences at birth, and the continued effects of heredity in the course of maturation, as well as any possible later effects of disease or injury, personality development might be regarded as successive transformations and vast-scale extensions through learning of features of behaviour present initially at birth. However, a great many different accounts have been given of the workings of this learning. One early view of personality development has been in terms of continued classical conditioning. (5) Less simplistic accounts have been those which include also forms of conditioning other than classical, and which pay special attention to the formation of new motives. (6, 7)

A potted version of the role of learning in personality development, consistent with the learning-theory tradition, might be somewhat as follows. Homeostatic functioning of organisms entails departures from equilibrium, that is, behaviour which is both varied and motivated. Some acts – those that lead to rewards – are reinforced, while others are not. The behavioural repertoire goes on increasing with maturation, while the moulding process of stamping in some modes of behaviour and not others continues unabated. A characteristic pattern of action, or the individual personality, gradually comes to be learned and gets firmly established. An important feature of this development is a process which could be called identification, whereby modes of behaviour of others are, as it were, taken over by the learning individual. This is said to be a vital ingredient of early learning, when the child tends to adopt parental attitudes, values etc. It occurs during the period of the infant's almost complete dependence on others. At that time gratification is almost entirely gained through the agency of the mother or mother-substitute, and therefore parent-like modes of behaviour and personality traits – or those that are acceptable to the parent – are the ones that are by far the most strongly reinforced. Also at that time the differentiation of male and female roles is sensed, the girl tending to identify with mother and the boy with the father. Thus, then, are the roots of every personality established.

Such an account of the role of early learning in personality development, though speculative, is consistent with, at least, some observations of infants. It may, of course, be greatly expanded and modified to suit different developmental psychologists' findings and outlooks. For example, the growth of the infant's inhibitory powers could be stressed; for the importance of 'impulse control, frustration tolerance, and delay of gratification' in personality development is beyond doubt. (8) The acquisition of these abilities through learning is a move towards advanced modes of functioning and a mature personality; and they are acquired whenever self-control, patience and waiting before acting are rewarded, as they often are in a normal family setting.

Some of the personality development is said to be associated with the earliest learning centred on feeding and excretory acts. In so far as feeding experiences are gratifying to the infant, the feeding mother – as well as other people (through stimulus generalization) – may become secondary reinforcers. The child will then seek the company of others and will gradually become sociable and socialized. If, however, feeding experiences are stressful, the mother's presence may acquire a stressful quality, which could be the basis for generally asocial or anti-social personality traits. The child whose hunger is satisfied contingent upon crying will quite likely learn different ways, and acquire different traits, from the one whose crying is not reinforced. (9) Bowel and bladder control have to be learned, and personality is said to be in part moulded by the character of toilet training. Training involving severe punishment may so stamp in conforming behaviour that, by generalization, a submissive personality will develop. Perhaps in some cases the child will take the parents' disgust with his being dirty for disgust with himself, and subsequently develop feelings of unworthiness and generalized guilt about himself. However, such different personality characteristics emerging from the various types of feeding experience and cleanliness training cannot be readily established by observation. (10) In fact, actual longitudinal studies of children cast doubt on the various predictions that have been made concerning personality-development repercussions of different infancy learning situations.

II.   Studies of non-human primates

Personality need not be regarded as a strictly human prerogative. 'Personality' differences among domestic animals – if one may put it that way – are often fairly obvious. It has been known for a long time that such differences can be brought about fairly readily by experimental means in such relatively lowly animals as rats. (11, 12) We saw in Chapter 5 how the reactivity of animals ranging from rat to monkey, and their later learning abilities, are influenced by conditions of rearing. We may now take this a little further by surveying some studies of 'personality' development in infra-human primates. A very great deal of the available information has come from studies of the rhesus monkey, and much of this emanates from the Primate Research Center at the University of Wisconsin and the Sub-Department of Animal Behaviour at the University of Cambridge. In point of fact the effects of early learning in monkeys and apes are for the most part inferred from the known effects of the deprivation of learning opportunities in infancy. The nature and extent of such deprivation may be relatively easily manipulated experimentally. Being reared more-or-less normally by mother and in the company of age peers is, of course, sure to involve a great deal of learning, which rather loosely may be called social learning. Prevention or restriction of such learning in monkeys has been shown to have quite a variety of effects.

Like children at some stages of their development young monkeys, when separated from their mothers, appear to respond with immediate distress which is later followed by a depression of mood. A subsequent re-union with the mother results in a marked and prolonged intensification of visible signs of attachment to her. (13, 14, 15) Unmothered female monkeys later make themselves poor mothers, being indifferent or abusive to their infants; and the sex behaviour of unmothered monkeys is at maturity both limited and abnormal in males and females alike. (16, 17) However, in the absence of mother, the company of other infants is most useful in the social learning of a young monkey – so much so that infant-infant interaction can in a large measure compensate the young animal for lack of mothering, at least in that it ensures in the motherless animals something like normal patterns in their later social and sexual behaviour. (18)

Monkeys kept from birth in social isolation for varying periods have been compared with captured feral animals. Animals so kept until early adolescence were subsequently found to be greatly handicapped in their ability to cope with environmental exigencies. They were found to prefer simple to complex visual and manipulatory stimuli; and in social contacts, such animals reacted with submission or flight. (19, 20, 21) When the length and severity of isolation had been systematically varied, findings were somewhat equivocal. For instance, the influence of early experience on the development of aggressive behaviour was not clear, although experience of a hostile mother proved to stimulate rather than suppress aggression later in life. On the whole the normal development of pre-adult behaviour seems to depend on the adequacy of early learning; (22) and this generalization, even though imprecise, may apply also to the human species, to which we must now return.

III. Early deprivation in children

Deprivation is a term used for a variety of conditions. It can refer to insufficiency of care and affection, to inadequate sensory stimulation, to separation from parents, to a poor cultural environment, and so forth. Some of the controversy surrounding the issue of deprivation in early childhood tends to vanish when the distinct effects of the different kinds of deprivation are investigated and analysed. Early deprivation does not necessarily entail a deficiency of early learning, but a great deal of deprivation can be seen in this light. Deprivation of care probably involves some restriction of learning. Deprivation of stimulation may be regarded primarily as 'drive frustration', but also – as a deficit of 'exposure learning' about the environment. And maternal deprivation, although representing an impoverishment of emotional life, also greatly limits the acquisition of specific attachments, of fears and of curiosity. Some writers take a more extreme view, and regard the effects of maternal deprivation as being wholly accountable in terms of early-learning events. (23)

It would be out of place to attempt here a survey of the quite vast literature concerned with the full range of effects of early deprivation in children. We must, however, pick out those strands within the mass of research which are of special interest in the context of the present chapter. Thus, we may first note that the initiators of research in this field – Spitz, Goldfarb, Bowlby – approached the issues from the psychoanalytic angle. They, therefore, laid stress on the emotional aspects of deprivation, namely on the deprivation of maternal affection and its consequences for personality development. However, before long observations of babies revealed that during the 'global stage' of development, roughly before the age of six months, the infant is not capable of a clear differentiation between mother and other people. If deprived of mothering, the infant will suffer perceptual rather than maternal deprivation. The latter can occur, whenever mothering is lacking, only during the later, 'differentiated stage' of development, i.e. in later rather than in early infancy. (24)

However, some writers go further than this, believing that maternal love is not, as such, a factor that influences behavioural development. The ill-effects of lack of mothering, such as are encountered in institutionalized children, are ascribed to insufficiency of stimulation, i.e. to deprivation which is perceptual rather than strictly maternal. (25) This could imply insufficiency of 'exposure learning' early in life rather than a lack of conventional conditioning. On the other hand, the view consistent both with the psychoanalytic and behaviourist traditions is that maternal deprivation diminishes opportunities for reward learning. For a deprived, nongratified infant will not develop behaviour patterns normally reinforced and established through good mothering. Thus, personality characteristics such as apathy, an interest in the self rather than the outer world, and even such traits as poor time sense, and limited imagination, might all be ascribed to inadequate infantile learning associated with maternal deprivation. (26)

It is important, however, to distinguish between those effects of early adversity which have to do with relatively short periods of separation from mother, and those that involve long-term deprivation of mothering. The effects of the former appear to be essentially reversible. The effects of the latter appear to be lasting, but are probably a good deal less severe than thought by earlier writers. (27, 28, 29) While a deficiency of early learning could handicap subsequent learning, it does not necessarily prevent a great deal of efficient later learning such as would ensure the development of what may loosely be described as effective and balanced personality.

IV. *Parental care and training*

Not all the aspects of parental care given to a child entail learning. Where care-giving results in the infant's learning, this is not by design. Training, on the other hand, deliberately sets out to bring about learning. Infant feeding could involve some training; elimination training sets out as such from the start, although it does not always produce quite the effects that are desired. Cleanliness training often entails punishment; so also does training in general good behaviour. While reward learning results in the establishment of generally stable habits, punishment training – though often highly effective – may have quite complex repercussions.

When modes of behaviour that are a natural expression of the infant, or that are gratifying in some way, are punished, the suppression of such behaviour may not be long lasting. Punishment may have to continue until the child develops some internal force suppressing the socially undesirable behaviour, that is, a self-control, described variously as conscience or super-ego. While the effects of punishment may be short-lived, they can at the same time be over-generalized, i.e. extended to situations markedly other than those in which punishment occurred. The punishing parent, as such, may become feared; and/or whole ranges of activity, such as eating, elimination, sex, etc, might be strenuously – if unsuccessfully – avoided by the punished child. Thus, the repercussions of parental training may be more extensive than intended.

Strict parental discipline, involving regular punishment of children, might be thought simply to suppress any tendency for rebelliousness in children. Empirical studies have refuted any such assumptions. (30) On the contrary, punishing parents may become models for aggressive behaviour in children, for imitative tendencies are pervasive in children's behaviour. Reasoning parents, too, may serve as models; possibly more so than punitive ones. For warmth in the parent-child relationship appears on the whole to facilitate imitative action, and may therefore be instrumental in the passing on of various personality traits from parent to child. However, our understanding of the effects of parental restrictiveness and permissiveness in different settings is very far from complete. (31)

The effects of inconsistent discipline are not quite clear either, although there is some evidence that such upbringing can make for later 'maladjustment'. Delay in rewards and punishments can render them ineffective; what is more, delayed reinforcement may build up uncalled for behaviour patterns, namely those which happen to have immediately preceded the events meant as reinforcements of earlier acts. Such unintended learning could contribute to the development of various idiosyncratic personality traits. It follows that punishment is probably most effective when it is applied in such a way that its termination is contingent upon the child's conformity. (9) A feasible alternative to punishing a child may sometimes be to reward it for doing something which is incompatible with the unwanted behaviour. While much training is clearly successful, the side-effects of care-giving and training by parents are various, and not always readily predictable. Early learning associated with these side-effects makes an undoubted contribution to the developing individual's personality.

V. *Early learning and later psychopathology*

Some of the acquired ways and traits fall within the range of normality, although what constitutes normal as against abnormal behaviour is in some considerable degree controversial. At any rate, some of the early learning is thought to be responsible for certain of the later abnormal modes of behaviour. But even those who look at the aetiology of abnormal behaviour primarily in terms of learning regard psychotic disorders as, at basis, constitutional. That is, it is thought that while some psychotic symptoms, such as delusions, are in a sense learned, the illness itself is not. It should be added parenthetically that environmentalist approaches which are more extreme regard even many psychoses as psychologically acquired. However this may be, it is relatively non-controversial to argue that neurotic disorders are acquired through learning, (32, 33) though it is very controversial in what sense of 'learning' they are acquired. Furthermore, it has also been said that criminality is largely learned. (34, 35) There is little doubt, of course, that learning early in life could play an important role in the development of neurotic and deviant modes of behaviour; what is arguable and uncertain is the precise nature of the learning which is implicated.

Now the 'learning approach' to neuroses holds that the origins of neurotic behaviour lie in the failure of the individual to acquire 'adaptive' responses and/or in his acquiring 'unadaptive' ones. An example of the latter would be some common phobias. These have been said to arise from coincidences of classical conditioning whereby a noxious stimulus is experienced shortly after some other stimulus; the latter thereby becomes conditioned and thereafter evokes irrational fears. Almost anything that occurs in the child's life could be involved in the formation of maladaptive 'habits'. It all depends on the occurrence of associations between various un-conditioned and conditioned stimuli, and the distribution of rewards and punishments in relation to everyday activities.

However, the habits and personality traits that have *not* been learned are said to account for psychopathy or amoral behaviour. For there are indications that psychopaths are, for constitutional reasons, difficult to condition and do not readily learn to avoid anti-social acts and to have regard for the welfare of others. While in some persons criminal behaviour may be due to such resistance to learning, in others criminality is said to arise from the absence of suitable opportunities for the early learning of morality. Persons in the latter category, while finding criminal acts rewarding, have not been punished for the initial criminal behaviour, or were pun-ished only after undue delay. Only extensive empirical studies can ultimately show to what extent this type of explanation of crimin-ality is justifiable.

Both the psychodynamic approach to the aetiology of neurosis, as well as the learning-theory approach, explain very many personality disorders in terms of early learning, the former view by implication while the latter – explicitly. Neurotic disorders have been cate-gorized into two types, dysthymia, and hysteria, and each has been said to be associated with certain conditions of conditioning. Dys-thymics are constitutionally introverted; they suffer from excessive anxiety which results from over-conditioning to which introverts are prone. Hysterics are constitutionally extraverted; they display various typical symptoms of hysteria resulting from under-condi-tioning which characterizes extraverted individuals.

This view relates in one way the constitutional and learning con-tributions to certain kinds of psychopathology. Any plausible account would, of course, attempt to explain abnormalities of per-sonality in terms of the interaction between heredity and environ-

ment. What is at issue is what precisely does happen, and especially
– because this is our theme – what kind of early learning can
account for later psychopathology. The learning-theory account is
acceptable where it fits the known facts. In many cases, however,
that type of account appears strained. For instance, the time relationships, known to be required for certain forms of conditioning,
often do not fit the actual case-histories of mental disorder. The
question is whether the known conditioning procedures are sufficient to explain what goes on during early learning. Could not
imprinting-like learning and various forms of 'no-trial' and 'one-
trial' learning be found a place in theories which explain individuality, normal and abnormal alike? But more about this – in the next
chapter.

NOTES

1   K. Lorenz, *Evolution and Modification of Behavior*, 1966, London:
    Methuen.
2   R. A. Hinde, *Animal Behaviour: a Synthesis of Ethology and
    Comparative Psychology*, 1966, New York: McGraw-Hill.
3   J. Bowlby, *Attachment and Loss*, Volume I, 1969, London:
    Hogarth Press.
4   P. Mussen, 'Early Socialization: Learning and Identification', in
    New Directions in Psychology III, 1967, New York: Holt, Rine-
    hart and Winston.
5   E. R. Guthrie, *The Psychology of Human Conflict*, 1938, New
    York: Harper.
6   D. C. McClelland, *Personality*, 1951, New York: William Sloane
    Associates.
7   A. Bandura and R. H. Walters, *Social Learning and Personality
    Development*, 1963, New York: Holt, Rinehart and Winston.
8   E. E. Maccoby, 'Early Learning and Personality', in *Early Educa-
    tion*, eds. R. D. Hess and R. M. Bear, 1968, Chicago: Aldine.
9   D. Jehu, *Learning Theory and Social Work*, 1967, London: Rout-
    ledge and Kegan Paul.
10 B. M. Caldwell, 'The Effects of Infant Care', in *Review of Child
    Development Research*, eds. M. L. Hoffman and L. W. Hoffman,
    1964, New York: Russell Sage.
11 J. McV. Hunt, 'The Effects of Infant Feeding-frustration upon
    Adult Hoarding in the Albino Rat', *J. Abn. Soc. Psychol.*, 1941,
    36, pp. 338–360.
12 J. McV. Hunt, H. Schlosberg, R. L. Solomon and E. Stellar,

'Studies of the Effects of Infantile Experience on Adult Behaviour in Rats', *J. Comp. Physiol. Psychol.*, 1947, *40*, 291–304.

13 B. Seay and H. F. Harlow, 'Maternal Separation in the Rhesus Monkey', *J. Nerv. Ment. Dis.*, 1965, *140*, pp. 434–441.

14 R. A. Hinde, Y. Spencer-Booth and M. Bruce, 'Effects of 6-day Maternal Deprivation on Rhesus Monkey Infants', *Nature*, 1966, *210*, pp. 1021–1023.

15 I. C. Kaufman and L. A. Rosenblum, 'Depression in Infant Monkeys Separated from their Mothers', *Science*, 1967, *155*, pp. 1030–1031.

16 B. Seay, B. K. Alexander and H. F. Harlow, 'Maternal Behavior of Socially Deprived Rhesus Monkeys', *J. Abn. Soc. Psychol.*, 1964, *69*, pp. 345–354.

17 H. F. Harlow, 'The Maternal Affectional System', in *Determinants of Infant Behaviour II*, ed. B. M. Foss, 1963, London: Methuen.

18 H. F. Harlow and M. K. Harlow, 'Social Deprivation in Monkeys', *Scient. Am.*, 1962, *207*, pp. 137–146.

19 W. A. Mason, 'The Effects of Social Restriction on the Behavior of Rhesus Monkeys', I, 'Free Social Behavior', *J. Comp. Physiol Psychol.*, 1960, *53*, pp. 582–589.

20 W. A. Mason, 'The Effects of Social Restriction on the Behavior of Rhesus Monkeys', II, 'Tests of Gregariousness', 1961, *J. Comp. Physiol. Psychol.*, 1961, *54*, pp. 287–290.

21 G. P. Sackett, 'Effects of Rearing Conditions upon the Behavior of Rhesus Monkey,' *Child Developm.*, 1965, *36*, pp. 855–868.

22 G. P. Sackett, 'Some Persistent Effects of Different Rearing Conditions on Preadult Social Behavior of Monkeys', *J. Comp. Physiol Psychol.*, 1967, *64*, pp. 263–265.

23 N. O'Connor, 'Children in Restricted Environments', in *Early Experience and Behavior*, eds. G. Newton and S. Levine, 1968, Springfield, Ill.: Thomas.

24 H. R. Schaffer, 'Objective Observations of Personality Development in Early Infancy', *Br. J. Med. Psychol.*, 1958, *31*, pp. 174–183.

25 L. Casler, 'Maternal Deprivation: a Critical Review of the Literature', *Monogr. Soc. Res. Child Developm.*, 1961, *26*, No. 2.

26 W. Goldfarb, 'Emotional and Intellectual Consequences of Psychologic Deprivation: a Revaluation', in *Psychopathology of Childhood*, eds. P. H. Hoch and J. Zubin, 1955, New York: Grune and Stratton.

27 N. O'Connor, 'The Evidence for the Permanently Disturbing Effects of Mother-child-Separation', *Acta Psychol.*, 1956, *12*, pp. 174–191.

28 M. D. Ainsworth *et al*, *Deprivation of Maternal Care: A Re-*

assessment of its Effects, 1962, Geneva: World Health Organization.

29 A. D. B. Clarke, 'Problems in Assessing the Later Effects of Early Experience', in *Foundations of Child Psychiatry*, ed. E. Miller, 1968, Oxford: Pergamon Press.

30 R. R. Sears, J. W. M. Whiting, V. Nowlis and P. S. Sears, 'Some Child-rearing Antecedents of Aggression and Dependency in Young Children', *Genet. Psychol. Monogr.*, 1953, 47, pp. 135–234.

31 C. W. Becker, 'Consequences of Different Kinds of Parental Discipline', in *Review of Child Development Research*, eds. M. L. Hoffman, and L. W. Hoffman, 1964, New York: Russell Sage.

32 H. J. Eysenck, *The Dynamics of Anxiety and Hysteria*, 1957, London: Routledge and Kegan Paul.

33 H. J. Eysenck and S. Rachman, *The Causes and Cures of Neurosis*, 1965, London: Routledge and Kegan Paul.

34 G. Trasler, *The Explanation of Criminality*, 1962, London: Routledge and Kegan Paul.

35 H. J. Eysenck, *Crime and Personality*, 1964, London: Routledge and Kegan Paul.

CHAPTER 10

Early Learning: Theorizing and Research

Development is a function of maturation and learning. These two are inseparable, for in a growing individual learning without maturation is inconceivable, and maturation without any learning at all would be, in fact, a most unlikely occurrence. Our own concern is the role of early learning in development, and hence the attention given in the last chapter to learning-theory accounts of development. This may have put an undue emphasis on the function of conditioning. By contrast, other approaches stress the importance of cognitive development. The so-called cognitive-developmental view, while acknowledging the role of learning, has as its central feature the doctrine of cognitive stage. (1) Such unfolding, successive stages in the development of children have been outlined by Piaget and, more recently, by Kohlberg. (2) The cognitive approach is undoubtedly an important one in developmental psychology, but a consideration of it would take us too far from the topic of early learning.

Yet another approach to the development of behaviour is that represented by Bowlby. (3) This emphasizes the central place in the development of animals and man of attachment behaviour. The role of learning in infancy is not minimized, but stress is laid on learning other than conventional conditioning. Attachment behaviour is not only central in early development; it is also considered to persist and to be of importance throughout life. Approaches of this type, like the cognitive-developmental view, help perhaps to counter-balance the traditional learning accounts of early development. This having been said, we must return to the topic of learning, and early learning in particular.

The very considerable difficulties encountered in attempting to define learning are well known. (4) Fortunately these difficulties have not seriously handicapped experimental work. We have already seen how various aspects of early learning have been studied in an effective manner. However, conceptual and theoretical questions cannot be entirely by-passed by experimentalists. It is, of course, not always possible to judge at the outset to what extent some theoretical problem will bear on attempts to gain factual knowledge. Having now reviewed empirical studies concerning early learning, we may pause and reflect upon the state of our knowledge. Such reflections will be the aim of the present chapter.

I. *One or more types of learning?*

An old problem of some interest to students of early learning is whether learning should be regarded as a distinct process or entity in some sense. That is, it may be sensibly asked whether theorizing about learning suggests that there is basically one kind, or more than one kind, of learning. Now, one way of classifying acts of learning would be to group them in accordance with certain outward similarities. Thus, one category would include verbal rote learning, another – the learning of manual skills, another – the learning how to behave, and so forth. Such classes, though useful in some ways, do not go down to the root of the problem; and various theoretical analyses of learning suggest other modes of classification. There are, however, many theories, and they themselves may be classified into types. This can be done according to different criteria, one of which is whether the theories postulate one or more kinds of learning. (5) But whether there are one or more kinds of learning is, in part, a matter of the level of analysis. (6) For instance, at a biochemical level all learning in all senses and of all kinds could involve the same processes, while at behavioural levels of analysis all manners of distinction might be made among learning situations.

While it is well known that learning theories may be classified into cognitive and stimulus-response theories, into contiguity and reinforcement theories, and so on, each theory is also more often than not quite explicit as to whether it holds that there is basically but one learning process, or two types of learning process, or several different types of learning. Single-process theories, whether or not specifying precisely the nature of this single process, have, naturally enough, always had a great appeal. Such theories have been propounded – among others – by Pavlov (7) and by Hull. (8) Two-process learning theories are typically those that stress the differences between classical (Pavlovian) and non-classical conditioning, asserting that all learning could ultimately be analysed into two such types of learning, and perhaps some combinations of them. The well-known exponents of this view have been Konorski, (9) Schlosberg, (10) Solomon and co-workers, (11) and some others. Those inclined to favour multi-process theories have been less outspoken and less explicit than the single- and two-process authors Examples here would be Tolman (12) (who may also be regarded as a single-process theorist), Thorpe, (13) and possibly all those others who see no great virtue in a well-rounded theoretical system whereby all learning is fitted into some clear-and-simple model. (14)

II.   *Varieties of training methods*

The question of the number of the ultimate processes of learning has its roots in the diversity of the training methods in existence. Among the training procedures used in the laboratory the best known ones are classical conditioning and operant conditioning; but there certainly are some others, which as procedures are clearly distinct. Avoidance conditioning may serve as example. In the interest of parsimony of explanation, attempts have been made to show that, on analysis, avoidance conditioning may consist of classical and instrumental learning, built in some way upon one another. Learning theorists have attempted to treat other training methods in the same way; but their reduction into elements of classical and/or instrumental conditioning often presents great difficulty. Now imprinting is a distinctive manner of animal training, even though at bottom it may have affinities to classical conditioning. Likewise, it is possible to teach subjects to imitate the behaviour of others, although here it could be argued that such learning ultimately consists of instrumental-conditioning sequences.

A training procedure of sorts is one in which an animal in the laboratory acquires fear as a result of some experimental treatment.

Fear of initially 'neutral' stimuli can be readily brought about by means of conditioning. Fear can also occur without prior learning in response to 'sensory deficit' (15) or to unusually intense stimuli. (13) (Needless to say, the specification of either level of stimulation raises some thorny problems, but this is not the place to discuss them.) Furthermore, it has long been apparent that some learning other than standard conditioning may be responsible for 'spontaneous' avoidance behaviour. (16) Indeed, the so-called incongruity hypothesis suggests that fear arises in cases of mismatch between current and past sensory inputs, or that current stimulation, having some common features with past stimulation but being also incongruous with it, arouses fear responses. (17) Thus, fear may be acquired in a variety of ways. Of course, fear may be defined in terms of a range of responses, and its definition could be highly controversial. Still, it is clear that fear may be implanted in subjects through training, and that an experimental analysis of such actual training into its component features need not necessarily be equivalent to a theoretical analysis of learning into its ultimate constituent elements.

Again, as we saw in Chapter 8, the early learning of language might be listed alongside other recognized 'training' procedures. The competence of the native speaker is probably gained not so much by dint of instruction, or reinforcing contingencies, as by the 'mere exposure' to the language. (18) The task of future research is to establish what precisely are the conditions of such exposure that are important in the initial learning to speak and, above all, to understand language.

We know that training situations such as pure classical conditioning or instrumental conditioning of one variety or another, or imprinting, and so forth, may occur at very early stages of life. We saw in Chapter 2 some of the evidence to indicate that classical conditioning can be brought about in various species soon after birth. We may well wonder whether emotional responses, classically conditioned, are perhaps the earliest responses learned, while learning to do things or to act in certain ways comes later. (19) However, some recent experimental evidence suggests that this may not, in fact, be the sequence. In monkeys, for instance, the ability to condition instrumentally to a noxious reinforcement develops rapidly in the infant. On the other hand, the ability to acquire emotional responses is a function of relatively slow maturation. (20) Again we may wonder whether imprintability is at its highest very early on, whereas conditionability is relatively poor at the start of life, improving steadily with maturation and with the development of 'learning sets'. Any such generalizations can only be confirmed or falsified by further developmentally directed research.

III. *Conditions of early learning*

Many academic psychologists see learning essentially as a re-organization of stimulus-response links. Others tend to regard learn-ing as, basically, a re-structuring of cognition. The latter notion may appear to be the more nebulous of the two, but it is at the same time conveniently flexible, being capable of varying interpretations. Cognitive re-structuring, conceived of as a central process, rather than as a sensory-motor peripheral process, could be envisaged as embracing both the 'impact' of sensory stimulation and the re-arrangement of the cognitive roots of activity. But how useful is it to regard learning as consisting of such inner-directed and outer-directed processes?

It has long been implied that it makes sense to distinguish within learning between the sensory-impact phase and the sensory-motor phase. Improved performance, changing habits, new modes of behaviour, and so on, are manifestations of the latter. Sensory or perceptual impact is harder to pin-point; but it may be inferred from such well-known experimental reports as those concerning 'latent learning' and 'sensory pre-conditioning', from studies of 'familiarity learning' involving the development of imprinted attach-ments and the consequent fear of novelty, and also from intro-spective reports of human subjects. The sensory-impact phase may be said to involve 'passive learning'; and this may, but need not, be reflected in subsequent performance. Although such learning may not be open to behavioural study in the short run, it makes sense to talk about it just because of such detectable long-run effects as shifts of preference, withdrawal from 'the incongruous', facilita-tion of later conditioning, and so forth.

The nature of the outcome of sensory impact or exposure learning depends on the characteristics of the stimulation as well as the motor potentialities of the organism. As an illustration of this point consider a young animal or a human infant that is exposed for a period to some colour. This could lead in some cases to an acquisition of a preference for that colour, or to an aversion to it. That is, under certain stimulus conditions the organism would exhibit attachment or avoidance behaviour, but because the organism is such as it is, it could not do much else. Now exposure to auditory stimuli, rather than visual, also allows in principle the development of a preference for, or an aversion to, the given sounds. But in certain cases it allows more than that, namely imitation.

The fact is that the potentialities of many species are such that exposure to sounds gives the individual more scope for delayed 'relevant' behaviour than exposure to visual stimuli. There are, of course, exceptions; the chameleon can, for instance, 'imitate' colours. However, the ability to imitate sounds is a great deal more widespread in nature; many birds are capable of it, and so are human beings. In fact, while exposure to particular sounds might result in a later preference for them, the more usual outcome is that the subject will produce sounds to match to a greater or lesser extent the sounds previously heard. Thus some stimuli provide more behavioural options than other stimuli.

Instead of, or in addition to, matching sounds the subject or observer may duplicate action. Imitation of behaviour is quite common among primates, and especially among the human species. In fact when an individual is exposed to some behaviour which is modelled, there is then hardly any scope for a shift of preference, as in the case of sounds, but only for imitation of the motor activity. Thus, whether exposure learning will result in imprinting, or imitation, or whatever the observable behaviour which appears to stem from the sensory impact may be, will depend on both the nature of the stimulation and the potentialities of the organism in question.

In operant conditioning responses are shaped by reinforcement to the point of forming virtually new modes of behaviour. In classical conditioning responses, though changing somewhat, remain essentially as before, but become attached to entirely new stimuli. In imprinting, and in shifts of preference through exposure, initial responses – somewhat as in classical conditioning – become attached to *any* stimuli within a certain range, but without any conventional reinforcement. In some forms of imitation, new responses emerge – somewhat as in operant conditioning – but their shaping is *guided*, although less closely than in the case of the so-called guided motor learning. Comparisons along these lines may be drawn between various known learning situations. It may be that the knowledge of early learning will advance not so much by the application of learning theories as by the study and experimental analysis of the circumstances of occurrence of the various early-learning events.

IV.   *Knowledge and speculation*

How much do we know about early learning and its later effects? The answer depends on what we are prepared to accept as knowledge; by liberal criteria, we know a great deal; by stringent ones, we know but very little. Statements made by eminent workers about transfer from early to later learning, about early personality development, or imprinting, or critical periods, often seem confidently knowledgeable. But criticisms of such 'knowledge' which are based on field observations, laboratory studies and clinical evidence have been no less trenchant.

As we saw in Chapter 1, Hebb proposed that learning undergoes important changes with age, and that, while slow, much early learning is permanent, providing the foundations for the more efficient, though often less durable, later learning. This is a generalization of a type capable, in principle, of being successively re-formulated with increasing degrees of precision. Some differences between learning abilities at different stages of development are known to exist; and some quite subtle differences between earlier and later learning have been revealed by experimental studies. However, it would be misguided to stake too much on such differences. Age is, after all, only one of very many parameters of learning. And it can be argued that differences between early and later learning are more quantitative than qualitative.

Freud was ostensibly concerned with early personality formation, although some personality theorists regard such development as, in essence, early learning. Freudian theory sees the development of personality as a function of natural growth and, above all, of learning to cope with frustrations and learning to resolve conflicts. To achieve these ends and reduce anxiety, the child adapts to reality situations by such mechanisms as displacement, sublimation, compensation, identification, the formation of defences, and so on. The initial motivational forces, or cathexes, gradually find new objects, and anti-cathexes which oppose instinctual urges are steadily built up. Is all this fact or fancy? It is not exactly either, but rather a set of interpretations of observable developments of behaviour. And only further empirical studies will enable us to judge whether such controversial interpretations make good sense or poor sense.

Lorenz, too, expressed himself rather unequivocally about certain developments in early behaviour. In describing imprinting in birds, he stated that the process is highly stable, or even irreversible, and that it is confined to a definite, brief critical period early in life. Reversibility can certainly be interpreted in more than one way, but in any case our present knowledge indicates that imprinting is not rigidly irreversible in any sense. Even the so-called critical period for imprinting has been seriously in question, and some quite severe qualifications of the term, critical period, as applied to imprinting, are necessary.

The critical period in relation to the socialization in animals has been much in the foreground in the writings of J. P. Scott. It has been said that if the opportunity for socialization is not provided at some specified time, proper socialization will never then take place. However, although there is evidence in favour of this view, especially from the study of dogs, the criticality of the time of taming and social learning has been repeatedly doubted or denied by research workers in this general field.

V. *Prospects*

All the various questionings, doubts and denials of definitive statements do not indicate that we have no reliable knowledge whatever of early learning. They mean, however, that we do not know enough to permit a single, defensible, 'big' theory to be put forward. Nevertheless, we certainly know enough to allow unambitious 'little' theories of early learning to flourish, that is, theories that confine themselves to relatively narrow ranges of behavioural events. Such theories are not only possible, they are necessary if successful research is to go on.

Are we then to dismiss altogether as valueless or even harmful the ambitious and essentially untestable theories? This would probably be too inflexible and dogmatic a stance to adopt. For, paradoxically, fanciful theories may have some scientific value. They can provide fresh similes and may thereby be instrumental in switching the researcher's thinking on to new rails. And this, in turn, may help the investigator to think of new hypothetical explanations of his findings which may then be empirically tested by further research.

Throughout the book we have been referring to useful limited-scale theories in various connections. Examples are ideas about the priority of development as between classical and instrumental conditionability, suggestions concerning the effects of primacy in early learning, the incongruity hypothesis of fear, hypotheses relating to sensitive periods in the development of behaviour, and so forth. Such theories have been particularly helpful in those areas of research in which experimental procedures are relatively simple and conditions are essentially controllable. This is so in some types of animal work; and, as published papers testify, there has been much tangible progress in recent years in the advancement of knowledge of animal behaviour. One would venture a guess that these developments will continue in the years to come.

There seem to be more obstacles in the path of progress in the field of early human learning. These are difficulties which are inherent in any experimental work with infants. Partly because of this much reliance has been placed in the past upon systematic non-experimental observations. However, results of observational studies are often susceptible to many interpretations; and the same set of observations could be grist to the mill of rival theories. In more recent years experimental ingenuity has led to 'tighter' studies of human infants; and some of the more recent findings and their theoretical implications are not readily disputable. So in this field of research, too, the outlook seems bright.

NOTES

1   L. Kohlberg, 'Stage and Sequence: the Cognitive-developmental Approach to Socialization', in *Handbook of Socialization Theory*

and Research, ed. D. A. Goslin, 1969, Chicago: Rand McNally and Co.

2   E. E. Maccoby, 'The Development of Moral Values and Behavior in Childhood', in *Socialization and Society*, ed. J. A. Clausen, 1968, Boston, Mass.: Little, Brown and Co.

3   J. Bowlby, *Attachment and Loss*, Vol. I, 1969, London: Hogarth Press.

4   G. A. Kimble, 'The Definition of Learning and Some Useful Distinctions', in *Foundations of Conditioning and Learning*, ed. G. A. Kimble, 1967, New York: Appleton-Century-Crofts.

5   E. R. Hilgard and G. H. Bower, *Theories of Learning*, 1966, New York: Appleton-Century-Crofts.

6   R. A. Hinde, *Animal Behaviour*, 1966, New York: McGraw-Hill.

7   I. P. Pavlov, *Selected Works*, 1955, London: Central Books.

8   C. L. Hull, *Principles of Behavior*, 1943, New Haven, Conn.: Yale University Press.

9   J. Konorski, *Conditioned Reflexes and Neuron Organization*, 1948, London: Cambridge University Press.

10   H. Schlosberg, 'The Relationship between Success and the Laws of Conditioning', *Psychol. Rev.*, 1937, *44*, pp. 379–394.

11   R. A. Rescorla and R. L. Solomon, 'Two-process Learning Theory', *Psychol. Rev.*, 1967, *74*, pp. 151–182.

12   E. C. Tolman, 'Principles of Purposive Behavior', in *Psychology, a Study of Science*, Vols. 1 and 2, ed. S. Koch, 1959, New York: McGraw-Hill.

13   W. H. Thorpe, *Learning and Instinct in Animals*, 1963, London: Methuen.

14   R. M. Gagné, *The Conditions of Learning*, 1967, New York: Holt, Rinehart and Winston.

15   D. O. Hebb, 'On the Nature of Fear', *Psychol. Rev.*, 1946, *53*, pp. 250–275.

16   R. Melzack, 'Irrational Fears in the Dog', *Canad. J. Psychol.*, 1952, *6*, pp. 141–147.

17   H. R. Schaffer, 'The onset of Fear of Strangers and the Incongruity Hypothesis', *J. Child Psychol. Psychiat.*, 1966, 7, pp. 95–106.

18   N. Chomsky, 'Explanatory Models in Linguistics', in *Logic, Methodology and Philosophy of Science*, ed. E. Nagel *et al*, 1962, Stanford, Calif.: Stanford University Press.

19   D. H. Mowrer, *Learning Theory and Behavior*, 1960, New York: Wiley.

20   G. W. Meier and C. Garcia-Rodriguez, 'Development of Conditioned Behaviors in the Infant Rhesus Monkey', *Psychol. Rep.*, 1966, *19*, pp. 1159–1169.

NAME INDEX

SUBJECT INDEX

GEORGE ALLEN & UNWIN LTD

Head Office:
40 Museum Street, London, W.C.1
Telephone: 01-405 8577

Sales, Distribution and Accounts Departments
Park Lane, Hemel Hempstead, Herts.
Telephone: 0442 3244

Athens: 7 Stadiou Street, Athens 125
Barbados: Rockley New Road, St. Lawerence 4
Bombay: 103/5 Fort Street, Bombay 1
Calcutta: 285J Bepin Behari Ganguli Street, Calcutta 12
Dacca: Alico Building, 18 Motijheel, Dacca 2
Hornsby, N.S.W.: Cnr. Bridge Road and Jersey Street, 2077
Ibadan: P.O. Box 62
Johannesburg: P.O. Box 23134, Joubert Park
Karachi: Karachi Chambers, McLeod Road, Karachi 2
Lahore: 22 Falettis' Hotel, Egerton Road
Madras: 2/18 Mount Road, Madras 2
Manila: P.O. Box 157, Quezon City, D-502
Mexico: Serapio Rendon 125, Mexico 4, D.F.
Nairobi: P.O. Box 30583
New Delhi: 4/21–22B Asaf Ali Road, New Delhi 1
Ontario: 2330 Midland Avenue, Agincourt
Singapore: 248C-6 Orchard Road, Singapore 9
Tokyo: C.P.O. Box 1728, Tokyo 100–91
Wellington: P.O. Box 1467, Wellington, New Zealand

MODELS OF THINKING

FRANK GEORGE

In this study the more logical types of human thinking are analysed – the ability to abstract, the development of concepts and so forth. Dr George describes the features that have long been regarded as central to thinking by experimental and theoretical psychologists and places a greater emphasis on the part played by language in cognitive affairs.

In the second part the author points out how such basic features of thinking as concept and hypothesis formation, inference making and the use of ordinary English are essentially things that can be carried out by a computer. His use of theories and his methods of modelling the human brain and the way it works comprise an intriguing and highly sophisticated attempt to provide an appropriate framework in which problems of thinking can be studied.

Complementing the author's graphic style are many drawings of great imaginative power by Anthony Ravielli. The artist worked closely with Dr. Elliott to depict accurately the various stages of the evolution of the brain.

THE SHAPE OF INTELLIGENCE

H. CHANDLER ELLIOTT

In his study Dr Elliott views the development of the human brain as 'the climax of a great saga, the tale of a quest for intelligence, for power to achieve and to experience'. He believes that this quest has been a steady and significant trend in evolution, persisting despite millions of experiments that have proved to be fatal errors or dead ends. Today man stands as the culmination, capable, more than any other creature, of coping with life and experiencing both its delights and frustrations.

To heighten the reader's understanding of the nature of intelligence, the author contrasts human life with other forms of life, pointing out the similarities and contrasts and making tangible the incredible series of events that have led to the development of the human brain. In an unusual appendix Dr Elliott presents an intriguing and unconventional account of life without nervous systems – life in the vegetable kingdom. A comprehensive glossary and index add further to the usefulness of the work.

INSTINCT IN MAN
RONALD FLETCHER

In this book, Dr Fletcher systematically examines the whole doctrine of human instincts and argues for the reinstatement of the theory of instincts in psychology. Three bodies of work are critically assessed: the work of the earlier psychologists, from Darwin onwards (James, Lloyd Morgan, MacDougall, Drever, and others); the recent findings of the Comparative Ethologists (Lorenz, Tinbergen, Thorpe, etc.) on instincts in animals; and the account of instinct given in Psychoanalysis. He demonstrates that these three bodies of work are not in conflict, but support and supplement each other, and then formulates a reliable and comprehensive theory of instincts. The more important implications which this theory has for other areas of study – such as education, social psychology, moral and social philosophy, and sociology – are discussed.

Most writers have approached the subject from one position only. Dr Fletcher gives a valuable assessment of every aspect. His thorough and up-to-date knowledge of the subject makes his excellent book a most useful contribution to literature on psychology.

MUIRHEAD LIBRARY OF PHILOSOPHY

MEMORY
BRIAN SMITH

In this book Dr Smith tries to bring together two lines of enquiry about memory: under what circumstances we are entitled to say we remember, and what is actually going on in us when we are remembering.

His aim is to discover how and why it is that we simply do have the same kind of certainty about many things in the past as we have about what is happening around us in the present; in short to discover the basis of the authority our memories have over us.

Dr Smith draws a distinction between memory-claims – the beliefs we assert about the past – and remembering – the experience which leads us and entitles us to make those claims. He then attempts to discover what kind of present experience is necessary for the making of what kind of claim about the past.

This involves a detailed consideration of the differences, and similarities, between remembering events, remembering how to do things and remembering our own past perceptual experiences, and leads to a full investigation of the nature of imagery and the relationship of imaging to remembering.

Whilst rejecting standard behaviourist accounts of memory as inadequate, he quite cheerfully embraces a mechanistic view of human thought and his theory of memory as it finally emerges is reminiscent of Locke's 'storehouse of ideas' – without the dualism.

THE NATURE OF THOUGHT

BRAND BLANSHARD

'It has been sixteen years in writing, and it is safe to say that here the problem of the function of thought has been discussed with such vigour and conciseness of language, such fullness of understanding and width of comprehension, that these two volumes are a model of what thinking about a subject really means.' *Church Times*

'Professor Blanshard is not only a philosopher of critical insight and constructive power; he also possesses a clear and pointed style and a happy knack of illustration. One cannot but remark on the useful detailed analysis, in the table of contents, of the argument of the book. Indeed, the author has spared no pains in the effort to aid the reader.' *Expository Times*

'I think it is one of the best and most important books written in the last few years in the field of philosophy.' A. C. EWING in *Mind*

'The author of this work . . . has produced a long and, within its appointed limits, an exhaustive treatise which is already of significance and which may prove to be fertile in its influence.' *The Times Literary Supplement*

'. . . a wealth of lucid exposition which does credit both to the clarity and the profundity of his thought . . . all students of philosophy will find them at once a strenuous exercise, a joy and an enlightenment' *The Inquirer*